EXPLORING
WEST YORKSHIRE'S
HISTORY

EXPLORING
WEST YORKSHIRE'S
HISTORY

NIGEL A. IBBOTSON

breedon **books**
PUBLISHING

First published in Great Britain in 2008 by

The Breedon Books Publishing Company Limited

Breedon House, 3 The Parker Centre, Derby, DE21 4SZ.

ISBN 978-1-85983-660-6

Printed and bound by Scotprint, Haddington, Scotland.

CONTENTS

INTRODUCTION

In 1974 the Local Government Act, which was passed two years earlier, had eventually come into force, changing the shape of many counties throughout England and Wales. Through this Act, West Yorkshire was born. The government of the day stated that it was not their intention to 'alter the traditional boundaries of counties, nor is it intended that the loyalties of people living in them will change, despite the different names adopted by the new administrative counties'. There are some things that legislation will never change nor erase, and those are our rich history and our pride in this land. Since the time of the Vikings, Yorkshire had been divided into three Ridings – West, East and North; with the West being the largest. The word Riding is derived from the Old Norse word 'Thrydings' meaning 'a third'. Each Riding was further sub-divided into administrative areas called 'wapentakes'. Literally meaning 'weapon take', the wapentakes (similar to the Anglo-Saxon Hundreds of Southern England) were originally meeting places, usually at a crossroads or near a river, where the freemen would assemble with their weapons to vote. Some sources suggest that it was by a show of weapons that the vote was carried out, whereas others have said that weapons were not flourished during the assembly, but collected at the end, hence the term 'wapentake'. The wapentakes had names such as Agbrigg, Osgoldcross and Skyrack, and references to them can still be found in West Yorkshire to this day.

Although significantly smaller than the West Riding, the metropolitan county of West Yorkshire still covers a considerable area, spanning more than 1,200 square miles, and has a population of around two million. West Yorkshire may be a relatively recent development, but the history of this land and its people spans a great expanse of time. Indeed, the story of the land beneath our feet stretches back hundreds of millions of years to a time before the dinosaurs roamed the earth. Great Seas flowed and ebbed, leaving layers of mud, which over time would harden into sandstone, limestone and millstone grit. Swamp lands replaced the seas, rich with tree ferns and giant mosses, which as they died and rotted formed layers of peat. Under great pressure, these layers would eventually form coal, which millions of years later would prove so vital to the Industrial Revolution. But, meanwhile, back in the mists of time our ancestors began to slowly tame the land, and with primitive tools they left their mark. Each generation that followed learnt new things, faced new challenges and also left their legacy.

The history of West Yorkshire has been made, not just by the rich, famous and powerful, but it is also the story of sweat and toil of the ordinary folk. It has been made by people with vision, industry and fortitude. By people small as well as the great, by the good and by the bad. West Yorkshire has left a rich legacy to the modern world through industry, the sciences, the arts and literature, and social reform. This history has been made by people who were not afraid to stand up and make a difference; people such as Richard Oastler, who worked tirelessly to better the conditions of children in the mills and was to spend three years in prison as a result of his beliefs. Sir Titus Salt, who was so concerned about the terrible pollution in Bradford, at one time reputed to be the dirtiest town in Europe, and determined to do something about it created his famous village at Saltaire. It was intended as a place where his workers could work and live in cleaner surroundings and consequently enjoy a better quality of life.

The county has also seen its fair share of battles, conflict and strife: the Battle of Winwaed in 655, the Battles of Wakefield & Ferrybridge during the Wars of the Roses and the numerous sieges, skirmishes and battles that raged throughout the region during the English Civil War. The late 18th and 19th centuries saw the Luddites protest and riot against the coming of the machines; the Chartists of the mid-19th century demanded rights and reforms for the working classes.

But it is perhaps for its undeniable position as world leader during the Industrial Revolution that West Yorkshire will be most remembered. Built upon the textile industry, its reputation grew to monumental heights. Its successes in the numerous subsidiary industries, such as engineering, mining and finance, have reinforced West Yorkshire's well deserved reputation. During our journey we will meet industrial giants, such as Edward Ackroyd, Benjamin Gott, Sir Titus Salt and John Fielden to name but a few.

As we travel around this diverse region we will discover that West Yorkshire is more than just a conglomeration of mill towns, but it also possesses a rich and varied landscape. Our journey will take us from the rugged foothills of the Pennines to the flat arable lands of the eastern side of the county. With breathtaking views that are sure to impress the observer, West Yorkshire offers a landscape that is as rich as its history and as rugged as the people who adorn the pages of our history books. This book is a journey through West Yorkshire in which we will explore the places and events that make up the region's exciting past – a journey that uses a combination of contemporary colour photographs and words to explore some of the well-known historical sites and some of the perhaps lesser known. I hope this book will encourage the reader to look deeper into what this wonderful county has to offer and to enjoy this journey as much as I have.

Nigel A. Ibbotson
May 2008

ACKNOWLEDGEMENTS

I should like to thank the following people, whose help has made this book possible. Firstly, I would like to thank my partner Kathryn, who has fully supported and encouraged me throughout this venture and has shown the patience of a saint. Also, I want to thank Mr Ernest Spacey for diligently reading the drafts and making many suggestions on content and grammar, and without whose invaluable contribution this book would have been markedly the poorer. Throughout my journey, either while collecting information or producing the photographs printed in this book, I have had the privilege of meeting many kind people who have assisted me in my quest. I would also like to thank the following people: Gillian Farr at St John's church, Halifax, for allowing me to photograph inside this wonderful building; David Adgar & Tim Charlson of the Churches Conservation Trust for allowing me to photograph inside the stunning All Souls church at Halifax; John Martin, the Press Officer at Harewood House; the Edinburgh Woollen Mill at the Haworth Weaving Shed; Steve Caron and Michelle Grainger at Breedon Books.

THE CITY OF LEEDS

Discovering the early history of a town or city is difficult and relies much on guesswork and conjecture, and understanding the origins of Leeds is no different. With little hard evidence, it is left to us to try and put some flesh on very scant bones. In prehistoric times the whole of the area would have been a combination of boggy marsh and dense forest. It is thought that in about 500BC the first early settlers started to make a small clearing in the woodland. We now know that this original site was near Leeds Bridge. Over time, increasingly more woodland was cleared until there were great swathes of farmland. The felled timber was used for shelter and fuel. Today the city of Leeds is one of the major metropolises; it is a vibrant place, with an exciting combination of outstanding old buildings and striking modern structures, which together guarantee that the city's rich legacy will continue far into the future.

EARLY RECORDS

In 731 the Venerable Bede, a Benedictine monk from Northumbria, completed his *Ecclesiastical History of the English People*, in which he describes a place he calls 'Loidis'. It is possible that he may have been referring to a region rather than a village or town. Part of the Kingdom of Elmet, it is thought that Loidis covered the land between present-day Crossgates and Aberford. According to Bede, the Battle of Winwaed took place in 655 in 'regio loidis' (in the region of Loidis). This 'bloody battle' was fought between King Oswy of Northumbria and King Penda of Mercia. At that time England was not one united country but was made up of a number of warring kingdoms led by warlords, each trying to gain the upper hand. By the mid-seventh century King Penda was in a position of supremacy, having allegedly slain at least six other kings by

his own hands. It is said that Penda was nothing less than a bloodthirsty heathen who worshipped the pagan god Woden and believed in human sacrifice. The Battle of Winwaed has been seen as a battle of good against evil; between Christianity and paganism. This maybe a rather simplistic view as, although there is no doubt that Penda was to remain a heathen throughout his life, he took a rather pragmatic view about Christianity. He even allowed four missionaries to spread the word of the gospel in his kingdom. He felt, however, that the followers of Christianity would let themselves down somewhat and often failed to practice what they preached.

The actual location of the Battle of Winwaed is unknown, but it is believed that it might have taken place at Whinmoor near Leeds, and there is good evidence to support this claim. Some believe, however, that when the Venerable Bede wrote about Winwaed he was actually referring to the River Went near Wakefield. The outcome of the battle was victory for the king of Northumbria and the death of Penda. Next to Barnbow Wood, which is a woodland area not far from Whinmoor, there lies a field called Pendas Fields. Could this field be the place that King Penda was slain? It is also thought that the name Whinmoor is derived from the Anglo-Saxon 'Winwaed'. We may never know for certain where the battle took place, unless further evidence can be found to shed light on either claim. One thing we can be certain of is that the reign of a tyrant was over.

All this does not, however, answer our initial question as to when Leeds first began as a settlement. Certainly, by the time of the Norman Conquest and the *Domesday Book* the village of Leeds had a population of 200, which meant that it would have been well established by the late 11th century. It was not, however,

Opposite:
The fountains in Millennium Square with Leeds Town Hall in the background.

until 1207 that a new town was established at the site of Leeds by the lord of the manor, Maurice De Gant. The Middle Ages was a time of rapid growth as trade and commerce began to flourish, resulting in many new towns being established. The manufacture of wool had become one of the main industries in Leeds. Not only was there a weekly market, but Leeds also benefited from two annual fairs. These fairs were important for the prosperity and growth of the town as they would attract people from all over Yorkshire either to sell their goods or buy from the local merchants.

BARWICK-IN-ELMET

There was once an ancient kingdom called Elmet that embraced the whole of West Yorkshire and beyond. Although evidence is very sparse, it is thought that Elmet extended from the head waters of the Humber to the foothills of the Pennines. As with all history from the Dark Ages, we have to rely on the

Hall Tower Hill at Barwick-in-Elmet, where a fort once stood.

writings of various monks such as the Venerable Bede and Gildas. In many cases these accounts were written years after the events – indeed, sometimes 100 years or more had passed before they were recorded. Other sources we have available to us are the limited archaeological findings. Occasionally, the only meagre evidence that we have left to us are the place names themselves. The so-called Dark Ages was a time of much change and upheaval, with migration, conflict and colonisation by the Anglo-Saxons (and later the Vikings), leading to the eventual re-naming of the country to 'Land of the Angles' – England.

In the early seventh century the Kingdom of Elmet was incorporated into the Kingdom of Northumbria when the Northunbrian King Edwin vanquished Cerdic (the last British king to rule this area). It is said that Edwin built a magnificent fortification at Barwick-in-Elmet, which covered an area of more than 13 acres. This was to be the seat of the Kings of

The ancient village cross at Barwick-in-Elmet; restored as a war memorial.

that proved to be a time of constant struggle between the Mercian king and the ruler of Northumbria. Eventually, as we have already discussed, Penda was defeated and killed at Winwaed. There is a stained glass window in the parish church of Barwick-in-Elmet that celebrates the victory of the Northumbrian king. The Venerable Bede wrote that the Northumbrian ruler had not only 'delivered his own people from the hostile depredations of the pagans and having cut off the wicked king's head, converted the Mercians and the adjacent provinces to the grace of the Christian faith.'

By the late eighth century Elmet's importance had started to wane as Offa of Mercia began to assert supremacy over the lesser kings and gradually brought the numerous kingdoms under his control. By marrying off his daughters to the rulers of Northumbria and Wessex he further strengthened his position, making him the first ruler to be truly called the 'King of the English'. The delightful village of Barwick-in-Elmet is no longer a seat of power for a kingdom, and the warring kings have long gone, but their stories will linger on.

Northumbria. It is thought that he built his royal mansion on a hill within the fortification, although no fragment of this building can be found to prove this. Hall Tower Hill stands near Barwick-in-Elmet, and it is thought that this was possibly the site where Edwin built his mansion. Edwin was eventually killed fighting the Mercian ruler Penda in 633 at the Battle of Hatfield Chase. This led to Penda ruling Edwin's lands for the next 20 years, a period

LEEDS CASTLE

The harsh and rugged landscape of West Yorkshire, particularly the closer you get to the Pennines, meant that the area was hardly suitable for agriculture and was mainly used for sheep farming. This led to West Yorkshire's long association with the textile industry. The ruggedness of the landscape also acted as a defence against armies, which tended to take other less taxing routes further east, and consequently very few castles can be found in West Yorkshire. The few that have been built have generally been situated on the eastern, flatter side of the region. Many centuries ago Leeds lay in the shadow of a castle. Today no trace of this stronghold remains. We do, however, know roughly where its keep would

THIS ANCIENT VILLAGE CROSS WAS RESTORED IN 1910 TO KEEP IN MEMORY THE MEN OF THIS VILLAGE WHO TOOK PART IN THE GREAT WAR 1914-1918 WHEN NEARLY ONE HUNDRED JOINED HIS MAJESTY'S FORCES AMONGST WHOM THOSE WHOSE NAMES ARE RECORDED ABOVE LAID DOWN THEIR LIVES

Plaque on village cross, Barwick-in-Elmet.

Now the Scarbrough Hotel, but probably the site where Leeds Castle once stood.

have stood, as a blue plaque attached to the present-day Scarbrough Hotel refers to a mediaeval manor house that once stood here surrounded by a moat. Further evidence that a castle once existed in this place can be found in the name, as it was called 'Castle Hill'. It is said that King Stephen laid siege to the castle at Leeds when travelling north to fight the Scots. In 1765 the manor house (the castle had long gone by this time) was rebuilt by Richard Wilson, and in 1823 it became Henry

Scarbrough's hotel. The present-day building, which stands near Leeds railway station, is a surviving extension.

KIRKSTALL ABBEY

Perhaps one of Leeds's most famous landmarks is that of Kirkstall Abbey. This evocative ruin, nestling on the banks of the River Aire, has long been a favourite with artists and photographers. Although standing in a truly picturesque and tranquil setting, this abbey has also been the scene of a troubled past. In 1147 a number of monks, under the leadership of a certain Abbot Alexander, left Fountains Abbey near Ripon to set up a new community. They first settled at Barnoldswick near Skipton on lands owned by Henry de Lacy, Baron of Pontefract; however, the conditions at Barnoldswick were harsh and, combined with much opposition from the local inhabitants, it soon became essential to find a new, more hospitable site. The Abbot found a stretch of land that was more suited to their needs, being well stocked with water, stone and

Plaque on Scarbrough Hotel.

LEEDS MANOR HOUSE

The medieval manor house stood here on 'Castle Hill'. Its deep moat looped between the river and Boar Lane. Richard Wilson lavishly rebuilt it in 1765 and in 1823 it became Henry Scarbrough's hotel. The present-day pub is a surviving extension.

timber. It was already inhabited by a group of hermits, who would eventually become incorporated into the community of monks. This stretch of land was Kirkstall, owned at the time by William of Poitou, a vassal of Henry de Lacy. Through the influence of the baron, Abbot Alexander was able to take possession of the land, and in 1152 the monks began to build their abbey, which they dedicated to the Virgin Mary. The original buildings were made of wood, but within a few years these were replaced with a more permanent structure of locally quarried gritstone. The work was surprisingly quick, and by the time of Abbot Alexander's death in 1182 the church, cloisters and surrounding buildings had all been completed.

Kirkstall was a Cistercian Abbey, and consequently the monks had taken a vow of poverty, chastity and obedience. Their robes were distinctive, being made of un-dyed white sheep's wool under a black cowl. The abbot, who was elected by the monks, commanded complete obedience and control over all aspects of religious and secular life. The life of the monk was hard and regimented, and there would have been little time for idleness as each day was interspersed by a number of services, the first Matins starting as early as 2am. When not at mass the monks would be working on the land or in the workshops, or perhaps involved with the instruction of the novices. The last abbot of Kirkstall Abbey was John Ripley, who had taken the post in 1528 and retired 11 years later. Throughout the abbey's history there had been 27 abbots in total.

According to a 15th-century document called *Fundacio Abbathie de Kyrkestall*, by 1301 the abbey owned 4,500 sheep and lambs. The importance of the flock could not be overestimated as wool was an extremely valuable commodity. In fact, for many centuries the crown would accept sacks of wool as payment of taxes, and even today the Lord Chancellor still sits on a wool sack in the House of Lords. The abbey would have easily found

The ruins of Kirkstall Abbey.

Doorway at Kirkstall Abbey.

customers for their wool as English wool was highly regarded throughout the continent and commanded good prices. Often they would sell the following year's production well in advance, and in 1292 they sold their wool in advance for the following 10 years – a highly risky gamble but one that brought in desperately needed funds. The abbey would have also found ready markets with its close neighbours Leeds and Bradford, whose main industry was the cloth trade. In all probability this would have had the knock-on effect of attracting even more weavers to the growing towns, therefore increasing the prosperity of Leeds, Bradford and of course the abbey itself.

Life at the abbey had never been completely without its troubles. As was common with other Cistercian communities of the period, their lives were often embroiled in legal difficulties over land and ownership; however, by the early 1530s their days were numbered. In 1531 Henry VIII had declared himself Supreme Head of the Church in England, and within

Opposite: Kirkstall Abbey in the dawn light.

three years he had coerced Parliament into authorising Thomas Cromwell to visit all the monasteries. This was under the pretext of confirming that the monks were instructed that the king was now head of the Church; however, the real reason was to take an inventory of the assets of all the monasteries, including that of Kirkstall. Reports began to filter back as to the scandalous affairs of the monasteries both of a financial and a moral nature. Relying on these reports of wrongdoings, Parliament passed a law that enabled the king to close all monasteries that had an annual income of less than £200 and to confiscate their assets. This lead to the Pilgrimage of Grace, an uprising that was to mainly centre on the counties of Yorkshire and Lincolnshire that had threatened the Crown for a number of weeks. Henry made a number of promises to the leaders of the rebellion to defuse the worsening situation. These concessions pacified the rebels long enough for him to regain control, and once he had done so he proceeded to execute the leaders. In 1539 a further law was passed giving him the rest of the monasteries in England. On 22 November of that year John Ripley surrendered Kirkstall Abbey to the commissioners of Henry VIII. It is said that the abbot then passed into retirement in the gatehouse and a number of monks were pensioned off.

Three years later the abbey and its lands were granted to the Archbishop of Canterbury Thomas Cranmer, only to be taken back by the Crown in 1556 when Cranmer was burnt to death for his beliefs. Over the following years the abbey was stripped of its roof, windows and stone, which was taken to use for local buildings. Some of the stone was used to construct the present Leeds Bridge. Little remains of what once would have been a magnificent building, but the ruins of Kirkstall Abbey still retain the power to capture our imagination.

BRIGGATE

The 'Road to the Bridge' (Brycg, old English for bridge, and Gata, old Norse for road) or as we know it today – Briggate, which is one of the main thoroughfares in Leeds, and as the name suggests it leads to a bridge. In 1207 the lord of the manor was granted a charter to create a new town. He built his new town on the street running north from a crossing on the River Aire. The charter gave him permission to divide the land into building plots, which he rented out for the sum of 16 pennies per plot per year. The plots were called a burgage, and there were 60 plots in total. Briggate was wide enough to hold markets and fairs. It is not known whether there was a bridge over the River Aire at the time when the street was laid out, but the name indicates that there possibly was. We know for certain, however, that there was a bridge by the 14th century. Over the years there had been a number of changes to it, but the bridge that can be seen today was built in 1871. Briggate is still at the heart of Leeds and is the location of a number of large department stores and well-known shops.

JOHN HARRISON

In Leeds City Square there stands a statue commemorating a very remarkable man: John Harrison. Born in 1579, he spent his entire life concerned with the welfare of Leeds and its inhabitants. After receiving a good education, possibly at the local grammar school, he went into business with his father. His father was a wealthy cloth merchant and when he died bequeathed John a substantial sum. With his inheritance he was able to buy a considerable amount of land. In 1624 John built a new grammar school on land of his own. This was to replace the old school, which was considered to be in an inconvenient place.

John was also instrumental in obtaining a Royal Charter from the king. After the charter was granted he became the alderman's deputy and was later to become alderman in his own right. In 1629 he joined a number of others to purchase the Manor of Leeds and bring it under the control of the Corporation. Renowned for his acts of generosity and his tireless work for the poor and needy, perhaps his best-known act of benefaction was the building of St John's

Leeds Bridge.

an interesting story that would suggest that he had Royalist sympathies during the Civil War. In 1647 Charles I had been imprisoned in Leeds, and John brought him a tankard that was thought to contain ale but was in fact filled with gold sovereigns. Other panels in the stained glass window depict some of his good works, such as building a row of almshouses for the poor next to the church. He also had a market cross erected at the top of Briggate.

THWAITE MILL

Throughout its history Thwaite Mill has had a number of uses. By the time it eventually ceased as a working mill in 1975 it was being used to produce putty, polish, pharmaceuticals and a number of other products that used ground flint, china stone and chalk. During World War Two the mill was kept extremely busy, producing putty to re-glaze London windows damaged throughout the Blitz. Originally the mill had started as a fulling mill in around 1641; however, little is really known of its history. What is known, though, is that the mill consisted of eight fulling stocks (large hammers that were used to pound the cloth) powered by four waterwheels. The location for the mill was ideal as it is flanked by the Aire and Calder Navigation in Stourton, Leeds.

The Aire and Calder Navigation Company purchased the mill in the 1820s and decided to redevelop the entire site. They employed a renowned millwright named Thomas Hewes to construct two large waterwheels and also to advise on the construction of the new mill. The project took two years to complete, and when it was finished the building stood two storeys high, complete with an engineer's workshop, warehouse, stables and a row of cottages for the workers. The total cost of the rebuilding was nearly £16,000. After the mill was reopened, it was first rented by a company that specialised in the production of rape oil, which was used for lubrication and lighting. It is said that the oil

Church. The church was built entirely at his own expense during the years 1631–1634.

The panels of one of the church windows depict various scenes from his life. One refers to

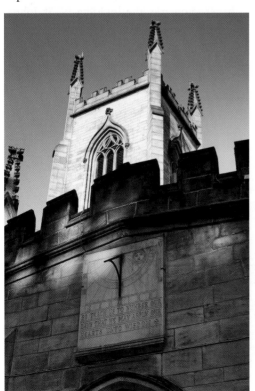

St John's Church – built by John Harrison.

used for lubricating Stephenson's *Rocket* was first produced here.

The mill has also been used for crushing exotic woods that had been imported from South America. The crushed wood was used as a colourant for dyes in the textile trade. For a short time the mill was also used to grind corn. The waterwheel and mill now belong to Leeds City Council and has been fully restored, complete with the manager's house. Thwaite House is a fine example of a Georgian house, built in 1823 on the foundation of an older house. The house overlooks the Aire and Calder Navigation, which not only provided a source a power to run the mill but also a means of transport.

LEEDS LIVERPOOL CANAL

Even though the Leeds Liverpool Canal was the first of the trans-Pennine canals to be started, it was the last to be finished and took 46 years to complete. In 1765 the canal had been proposed for the transportation of woollen goods from Leeds and Bradford, but it was not until five years later that work commenced on the first stage of the canal. Although the Lancashire backers had understandably pressed for work to start at Liverpool, the first stage to be completed

was from Skipton to Bingley, as this stretch was to be lock free. Over the years the canal was completed in stages as the funds were raised to continue with the work. Bingley was to become the site of the famous Five Rise Staircase lock.

During the 19th century the canal prospered, as it was one of the main methods of transporting goods such as coal, stone and textiles. The introduction of the railway network appears to have had little impact on the popularity of the canal, and it was only the coming of heavy goods vehicles and road transport that eventually caused its demise. Today it is rare to see goods transported by canal; however, by the latter part of the 20th century many canals had been renovated, including the Leeds Liverpool Canal, and they have become popular for leisure pursuits. There are now many boatyards and marinas along the canal, catering for this growing trend.

BEAN ING MILL

Today the present *Yorkshire Post* building is situated where Benjamin Gott's Bean Ing Mill once stood. Sadly the mill is no longer there, but Gott's legacy remains as one of the pioneers of the Industrial Revolution. Traditionally,

Five Rise locks at Bingley – the first section of the Leeds Liverpool canal to be opened, it was started in Shipley and ended in Bingley.

cloth had been produced in rural cottages in villages throughout West Yorkshire. As the various stages were undertaken at different places, much time was wasted and costs incurred in transporting goods back and forth throughout the region. Another disadvantage to this cottage industry was that the whole process took about 29 stages to produce the finished cloth, and quality control was a major issue, often resulting in a low-quality, rough cloth. It was Benjamin Gott who first saw the advantage of having all these processes under one roof so as to control the manufacture from beginning to end, therefore maintaining a consistent quality.

Born in 1762, Benjamin was the son of a civil engineer called John Gott from Calverley. After receiving an education at Bingley Grammar School, he was apprenticed at the age of 18 to John Wormald and Joseph Fountaine, a partnership of woollen cloth merchants based in Leeds. He became junior partner in 1785, and within a relatively short time both of the other partners died, leaving him in control.

Benjamin was still a relatively young man when, at the age of 30, he was to embark on his ambitious plan to build a mill that would accommodate all the stages in the process of making cloth. Purchasing 16 acres of land just west of Leeds along the River Aire at Bean Ing, he built his mill. Moving all the stages under one roof not only saved him time, but he was also able to maintain better quality control. Although this was a marked improvement in the production of cloth, it was still produced totally by hand. What was needed was mechanisation to increase the mill's efficiency even further. At first he used a waterwheel to power the mill, but the location was not ideal for water (as the flow of water at that site was inadequate), therefore he had to look for another method of powering the mill. To solve his problem he purchased a coal-fired steam engine from a London firm called Boulton &

Calls Landing on the banks of the Aire and Calder Navigation. Opened in 1700, before the arrival of the age of the railway, water was essential for cheap and efficient transport.

Watt. He was to have both the first beam and steam engines in Yorkshire. These machines, however, proved too delicate to make the journey up to Yorkshire, so his only alternative was to have them built locally. Buying the patent, he was to have them fabricated in Batley.

By the time of his death in 1840 the Industrial Revolution was drawing to a close, and Benjamin Gott had not only witnessed a dramatic change in the woollen trade from a cottage industry into a fully mechanised and world-class industry, but he had also played an instrumental part in its creation. He also had much in common with all the other industrial pioneers of the early and mid-19th century, such as Sir Titus Salt, Edward Akroyd, Lord Masham and John Fielden to name but a few, in that he was a canny businessman and philanthropist who was generous with his wealth. He was a patron to the arts and one of the founders of the Leeds Philosophical and Literary Society.

The Corn Exchange.

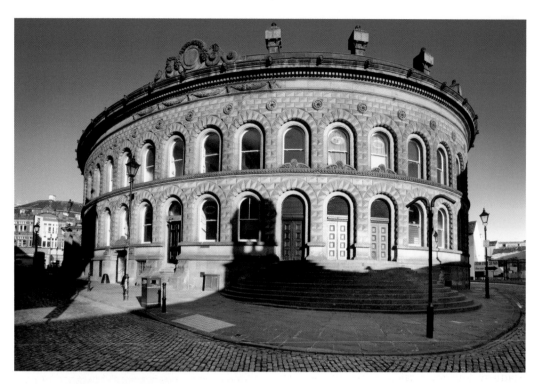

THE CORN EXCHANGE

Some consider the Corn Exchange to be one of the finest examples of a Victorian building in Britain. Construction on this outstanding building was completed in 1864 and was the work of Cuthbert Brodrick, a young architect from Hull who had already gained international recognition with his design for Leeds Town Hall, which had been built six years earlier. It was constructed as a place where merchants came to trade in corn and cereals. The large oval hall was lit by windows in the roof so as to make the grading of corn easier. Along with Leeds Town Hall and Kirkstall Abbey, it is perhaps one

Leeds Town Hall in the early morning light.

of Leeds's most recognisable buildings. Today it houses a variety of fashionable shops selling clothes and jewellery.

TEMPLE MILL

Perhaps one of the most unusual mills to be built in the 19th century was John Marshall's Temple Mill, which was constructed to replicate an Egyptian temple. Born in 1765, the son of a linen draper in Leeds, he was to inherit the family business at the tender age of 22. John Marshall was keen to expand the business into flax spinning and bought the patented rights for machinery to spin the flax. He established his factory at Scotland Mill at Adel with his partners Samuel Fenton and Ralph Dearlove. Due to his lack of experience and knowledge, the business was to struggle until he met Matthew Murray, a talented young engineer. Together they managed to create an efficient flax-spinning machine. In 1792 the operation was moved to Water Lane in Holbeck beside a beck, which they used as a source of power. The following year his partners had totally lost confidence in the enterprise and withdrew their support, which meant that Marshall was forced

Detail of Temple Mill.

to look for new investors. He was able to find this support in the form of two brothers called Benjamin and Thomas Benyon. This, however, also proved not to be a smooth relationship so, raising enough capital, he was able to buy them out in 1804.

The stunningly ornate Temple Mill with a red brick mill in background.

Improvements in steam power made by Matthew Murray meant that water was no longer required to be pumped directly from the beck, enabling Marshall to move his factory to a better location on the other side of Water Lane, which was less liable to flooding. There followed a period of prosperity, especially as there was an increased demand for cotton and flax fibres throughout the war with France. Over time he brought both his sons into the business, but it was his youngest, James Garth Marshall, who was to have a profound influence on the growth of the business.

In 1838 John Marshall started work on his last mill, the iconic Temple Mill. This mill was designed by Joseph Bonomi and was seen as the crowning glory of John Marshall's career. The new mill was based on a number of Egyptian temples but most notably the Temple of Horus at Edfu. The building was years ahead of its time and had a number of unusual features, including a grassed roof, which aimed to keep in the humidity needed for flax spinning. John Marshall died in 1845, and sadly the business

ceased to trade a number of years later in 1886 when no one was willing to continue the family firm. Fortunately, this stunningly ornate building still stands as a memorial to Victorian endeavour and workmanship.

THORNTON'S ARCADE

Leeds has a number of fine arcades, the first to be built being Thornton's Arcade. It was built in 1878 by Charles Thornton, the owner of the Old White Swan on Swan Street and the Varieties Music Hall (now known as Leeds City Varieties). The arcade was erected on the site of the Old Talbot Inn. The Talbot had been one of the oldest public houses in Leeds. It had been used for cockfighting, and the circuit judge in the 17th century had used it as a place to stay when visiting Leeds. The walls of the inn had been covered in frescoes, which were described by the 18th-century historian, Ralph Thoresby, in his book *Ducatus Leodiensis; or the Topography of the ancient and populous Town and Parish of Leedes and parts adjacent in the West Riding of the County of York*. Described in

Entrance to Thornton's Arcade.

Far left: Clock in Thornton's Arcade, with figures from Ivanhoe.

Thornton's Arcade.

the Victorian publication *The Gentleman's Magazine* as 'a man of insatiable curiosity', Thoresby was to gain fame as a great antiquarian and is regarded to be the first historian of Leeds.

The initial plans for the arcade were designed by Charles Fowler. Due to problems with the drainage the plans failed to get approval from the borough engineer, and Charles Thornton was forced to replace his architect. The task of altering the plans to get approval fell to the architect George Smith, and in May of 1878 the arcade was officially opened.

One of its most remarkable features is the clock located at the west end of the arcade. The mechanism for the clock was made by a local firm, William Potts and Sons of Leeds, and the figures that still strike the bell were the work of Leeds sculptor, John Wormald Appleyard. The figures are based on characters from *Ivanhoe* by Sir Walter Scott: Richard the Lionheart, Friar Tuck, Robin Hood and Gurth the Swineherd. At the other end of the arcade can be found the sculptured head of a young woman, complete

with long flowing locks and a large hat, which was based on the painting of the Duchess of Devonshire by Gainsborough. Leeds possesses a number of elegant arcades, all built in the latter part of the 19th century: Queens Arcade (1888–89), The Grand Arcade (1898), County Arcade and Cross Arcade (1898–1903) respectively. Today all these arcades have been restored and are an integral part of the Leeds shopping experience.

Sculptured head in the style of a Gainsborough painting.

SCULPTURES IN LEEDS

Leeds boasts a fine collection of sculptures, which are located throughout the city. The first sculpture that the visitor is to meet as they leave the City Station is that of the Black Prince, who stands proudly in City Square. This was a gift from Colonel Thomas Walter Harding, who had been lord mayor of Leeds between 1898–99. Although the Prince had no connection to the city of Leeds, Harding felt that the son of Edward III symbolised the virtues of democracy and chivalry.

Guarding the town hall are four white lions, which are thought to have been inspired by the lions around Nelson's Column. The lions were the work of William Keyworth and were added to the town hall nine years after it was built. Legend has it that, as the clock strikes 12, the lions get up and walk around the building before resuming their positions. A little further up from the town hall is Leeds City Art Gallery, with its famous statue by Henry Moore reclining at the entrance.

LEEDS CIVIC HALL

This stunning building was opened on 23 August 1933 by King George V. The Leeds Civic Hall houses the council, which is composed of

99 councillors. It includes the lord mayor's office, council chambers and banqueting hall. Built during the Great Depression, it had been a job creation scheme of its day using unemployed workers to construct it. The building was designed by the English architect Emanuel Vincent Harris, who was chosen as the winner of a competition held in 1926 to design the hall.

The building is guarded by two magnificent golden owls standing on columns, the owl being the emblem of Leeds. Behind them are two equally exquisite gold clocks, and together in the bright sunlight they all make a truly wonderful sight. This impressive building overlooks Millennium Square, which was opened in December 2000 and is home to several large pieces of public art.

The Black Prince in City Square.

The golden owl and clock of the Civic Hall.

It was after completing the Eddystone Lighthouse that he decided to pursue the lucrative career of civil engineering. He undertook a number of projects, including the Calder and Hebble Navigation. It was through his expertise in the field that he was to be the expert witness to appear in an English court, when he was called to testify in a court case relating to the silting up of the harbour at Wells-next-the-Sea in Norfolk. It was John Smeaton who came up with the term 'civil engineers' as to distinguish them from the military engineers who were graduating from the Royal Military Academy at Woolwich. John Smeaton died on 28 October 1792 after suffering a stroke while walking in the garden of his family home, and is buried in the Whitkirk Parish church near Leeds. Near Austhorpe is a school that has taken his name, and his fame lives on, having recently been mentioned in the song *I Predict a Riot* by the pop group Kaiser Chiefs, who also come from Leeds.

JOHN SMEATON

Regarded as the father of civil engineering, John Smeaton was born on 8 June 1724 at Austhorpe in Leeds. Educated at Leeds Grammar School, he started his working life at his father's law firm. He had little interest in law and was soon to leave to become a mathematical instrument maker and work with Henry Hindley, who was famed for building the clock in York Minster. In 1753 John Smeaton was elected a Fellow of the Royal Society, and six years later he won the Copley Medal for his research into the mechanics of waterwheels and windmills. He is credited with inventing the cast-iron axle shaft for waterwheels. He is perhaps most famous for designing the Eddystone Lighthouse, a commission he received on recommendation from the Royal Society. While building the lighthouse he developed a technique of dovetailing the blocks of granite. His pioneering work on 'hydraulic lime' (a form of mortar that will set under water) eventually led to the development of Portland cement.

ILKLEY

On the edge of the Yorkshire Dales is the delightful spa town of Ilkley. This spa town, once called Heather Spa (a reference to the vegetation on the surrounding moors), has an ancient history going back to the Mesolithic period, about 11,000BC. There has been a known settlement at Ilkley since the early Bronze Age. The surrounding area is rich in evidence of early man's activities, and more than 250 cup and ring markings having been found on the rocks. Perhaps one of Ilkley's better known and impressive early carvings is the Swastika Stone, located on Woodhouse Crag overlooking Ilkley. It is not known how old the carving is, but it is certainly thought to be as old as the cup and ring markings, which date between 2800 and 500BC. The name Swastika is derived from the Sanskrit word 'svastika' meaning a lucky object or literally 'little thing associated with well-being'. The symbol can be found throughout the ancient world. Sadly, it was to receive bad press through

*The dramatic
Ilkley Moor.*

its use by the Third Reich, and today it still has evil connotations.

According to a book by Rev. Robert Collyer and J. Horsfall Turner, published in 1885, 'good scholars imagine' that Ilkley takes its name from 'Llecan', the old British name for rock. During the Romano-British period the Romans built a fort at Ilkley, which it is generally accepted was called Olicana (however, this name is now in debate as it is thought by some that it was a scribal error and its real name was Verbeia, which was the Roman name for the River Wharfe). As the Romans were the bureaucrats of the ancient world and well known for keeping records, no matter how trivial, it seems probable that for the most part the garrison at Ilkley would have had a fairly quiet time of it as there are no Roman chronicles of any military events in the locality. It is quite possible, though, that Ilkley was embroiled in the troubles of AD180 when the Scots ventured south and created havoc among the inhabitants of Yorkshire.

Ilkley developed into a spa town in the 18th and 19th centuries and, according to a letter written by a certain Dr Richardson in around 1709, 'Ilkley now is a very mean place, and is equally dirty and insignificant, and chiefly famous for a cold well, which has done very remarkable cures in scrofulous cases by bathing, and in drinking of it.' It appears, though, that the spa at Ilkley was newly discovered as Ralph Thoresby, author and antiquarian and, as we have already mentioned above, credited as being the first historian of Leeds, made no mention of it as he passed through Ilkley in 1694. He had a particular interest in springs and spas, therefore it is highly likely that if the existence of a spring had been known at this time he would have at least mentioned it in passing. It is known that a primitive well stood in the proximity of the spring head before the famous White Wells Spa, complete with baths and dressing-rooms, was built by William Middleton at the end of the 18th century. It was at this primitive well that a tragic event happened in 1793 when Ann Harper, the local butcher's nine-year-old daughter, drowned while trying to bathe in the well.

With the introduction of hydropathy, a pseudoscientific method of treating diseases with the use of water, in 1843 a number of

Waterfall at Heber's Ghyll, near the Swastika Stone.

Overleaf: Cow and Calf at Ilkley.

White Wells at Ilkley.

establishments were built in Ilkley, taking advantage of its spring water. The Ben Rhydding Hydropathic Establishment was the first to be built in 1846 by Hamer Stansfield, and its first physician was a Silesian named Dr Rischanek who was replaced the following year by the celebrated Dr MacLeod. This establishment was followed by Wells House, Craiglands, Troutbeck and Rockwood House to name but a few.

The moor, with its renowned Cow and Calf, the great gritstone rocks, rises 1,319ft above sea level. It is said that the famous song (and unofficial anthem of Yorkshire) *On Ilkla Moor baht 'at* was improvised by a choir from Halifax while picnicking by the Cow and Calf.

(Chorus)
Wheear 'as tha bin since ah saw thee?
On Ilkla Moor Baht 'at
Wheear 'as tha bin since ah saw thee?
Wheear 'as tha bin since ah saw thee?
On Ilkla Moor Baht 'at
On Ilkla Moor Baht 'at

Sign on the side of the Hermit public house.

On Ilkla Moor Baht 'at
(Verses)
Tha's bin a courting' Mary Jane
Tha's bahn t'catch thi deeath o'cowd
Then we shall ha' to bury thee
Then t'worms'll cum and eat thee oop
Then ducks 'll cum and eat oop t'worms
Then we shall go an' ate oop ducks
Then we shall all 'ave etten thee

THE HERMIT OF ROMBALD'S MOOR

Take the picturesque road to Ilkley and you are sure to pass the famous hostelry called The Hermit. This place is named after Job Senior, a colourful character whose reputation as a singer, soothsayer and weather forecaster was well known throughout the area during the 19th century. Born around 1790, it is said that he was the illegitimate son of a wealthy landowner from Ilkley; a story that was given some credence, for there appeared to be little contact with a father figure in the young Job's life. It is known that his surname was that of his unmarried mother. Very little is known of his childhood other than he was to grow into a strapping youth with good looks and a ready wit.

Whoever his father was, there appeared to be a rather belated gesture of remorse, as Job was to receive a legacy, which he used to fuel his drinking habit. Offering his service as a labourer to the local farmers, he made a somewhat precarious living and became well

acquainted with the taverns throughout the area. For a time he considered settling down when a young lady at Whitkirk caught his eye, but his advances were to be rejected, and it was not long before he resumed his dissolute ways. His heavy drinking was to cost him a number of jobs, and he was soon reduced to poverty.

Job was a sorry sight, dressed in rags and racked with rheumatism; he turned to singing in the taverns to make a few pence. He possessed a remarkable voice, and it was claimed that he was the only man able to sing treble, alto, tenor and bass. It was not long before his achievement brought him invitations to sing in the theatres of Leeds and Bradford. He performed to packed audiences, and his talent brought him much attention. It appears that his earlier lack of success with romance did not entirely put him off, and when he reached 60 he met and married a widow 20 years his senior. His bride possessed a comfortably furnished cottage, which he saw as insurance for his own old age as he concluded that he would in all probability outlive her. Job was correct in his assumption, and she died a short time after they were married. There was a shroud of mystery around the circumstances of her death, and some say that he helped on her way to profit from her will. Whatever the cause of her demise, her relatives were angered when they realised that all her property would pass into his hands. Waiting until Job was away from the cottage; they broke in and removed everything, razing the ransacked house to the ground. All that was left was a heap of stones and broken timber. From the pile of debris Job built a small shelter, no larger than an outsized dog kennel, which he would enter on all fours.

It was from that moment he became known as the Hermit of Rombald's Moor, and sightseers came from all over to see the spectacle of the ragged recluse. A battered hat upon his head hid much of his matted uncut hair, his clothes were a mass of patches and straw was wrapped around his legs. His pipe dangled on a string from the brim of his hat. To survive he toured the district and sang. It was at this time that he was to become known as a soothsayer, and young men would visit him to ask his advice on matters of the heart. His stock answer was to practice celibacy and be content with single life. In 1857, while out walking, he was struck down with an illness, which caused him to go to Ilkley, the town of his birth. It transpired that he had contracted cholera, which at that time had reached epidemic proportions in the district. He was taken to a workhouse, where a short time later he passed away. It is said that his end had been aided by a couple of youths who had drugged his ale while he had been drinking at a Silsden inn, and this had weakened his resistance to the disease. Today a public house called the Hermit can be found at Burley Woodhead near Ilkley. Once called the Woolpack, it had served drovers of pack ponies carrying wool to Bradford. Job would have been well acquainted with this hostelry, and it has changed little from his day.

OTLEY

Dating from before Roman times, Otley is a town close to Leeds and formed an important crossing point on the River Wharfe. It was one of the great Saxon parishes, and its importance was recognised in that it was the administrative centre of the wapentake of Skyrack during the Middle Ages and became the seat of the Mid-Wharfedale Urban District council until the reorganisation of 1974. Otley Parish Church was built on the site of an earlier seventh-century church and houses the remains of two early Anglo-Saxon crosses. In the churchyard lie the remains of an ancestor of Henry Wadsworth Longfellow, the 19th-century American poet, and also the grandparents of Thomas Fairfax who commanded the Parliamentarian forces at the Battle of Marston Moor in 1644.

Otley is a traditional market town that is

Paper mill and weir at Otley – the area was renowned for the production of paper.

unquestionably a beauty spot within a very picturesque setting. It is perhaps difficult to imagine today, but after the Norman Conquest the Borough of Otley was markedly larger than its neighbour, Bradford, and by the late 13th century it was sending two members to Parliament. Possibly due to its connections with the Fairfax family, Otley supported the Parliamentarians during the English Civil War. It appears, though, that their loyalty was split, as legend has it that while the Roundheads were drinking the town dry on the eve of the Battle of Marston, Prince Rupert's Cavalry were allowed to graze their horses on the slopes of the Chevin.

In 1797 the famous painter, J.M.W. Turner first visited Otley when he had been commissioned to paint a series of watercolours. He was so taken with the area that he was to return many times. Another frequent visitor to Otley was the Methodist preacher John Wesley, and one of the main streets of Otley is still named after him. In 1856 a local firm called Dawson, Payne and Elliot revolutionised the

printing press when they built their first 'Wharfedale Printing Machine'. Initially they had called it 'Our Own Kind', but, because they had failed to take a patent out on the machine, it was inevitably copied by firms throughout the world. Rivals would go to great lengths to headhunt Dawson's employees to show them how it was built. Even so, the 'Wharfedale' dominated world markets up to modern times, and as late as 1965 an order was placed for 28 of the machines to produce copies of the Holy Koran in Pakistan.

THE CHEVIN

High above Otley is the Chevin Forest Park, with its breathtaking views of the Wharfe Valley. This woodland escarpment has massive rock outcrops that rise steeply to a height over 900ft above sea level. It is said the Chevin derived its name from the Celtic word 'Cefyn' or 'Cefu', which means ridge – a very apt name indeed.

The Chevin took millions of years to form, and its story began even before dinosaurs roamed the earth. Periodically the level of the sea would rise and fall and these fluctuations would leave thin layers of mud. Over millions of years, due to great pressure, these deposits would harden to become Carboniferous Millstone Grit. It was this hard rock quarried from the Chevin, that was used for the foundations of the Houses of Parliament. Even today fossils of marine life can be found in the rocks of the Chevin, which is further evidence of its watery past. Over time, as the continents moved and collided, a ridge was formed from Addingham to Harewood, the Chevin being part of this long ridge.

With the coming of the Ice Age the whole area was covered with a thick layer of ice, and the Wharfedale glacier reshaped the land once again. Evidence of the devastating power of the glacier can be seen in the form of the great blocks of limestone that were dragged from the north of Yorkshire and deposited at Reva near

The sun setting on Surprise View, the Chevin.

Menston. It is possible that woolly mammoths and woolly rhinos had roamed this icy tundra, but we cannot be sure. What we do know, however, is that as the ice receded the area became rich in animal life such as wild horses, red deer, giant ox and wild pigs that roamed the area and would have offered bountiful hunting grounds for the hunter-gatherers of the Palaeolithic Age.

The Chevin is an extremely popular tourist spot and Surprise View, its highest point, offers stunning panoramic views of up to nearly 40 miles on a clear day. There are a number of paths throughout the forest park; however, all the routes can be described as being at best challenging, as all are steep in places.

DENTON HALL

The Denton Estate has a long history dating back to the middle of the 13th century when it was owned by a certain Athelstan. Over the years it changed hands a number of times until in 1515 the Fairfax family became the new owners. It was the third Lord Fairfax, Thomas, also known as 'Black Tom' due to his dark complexion, who was to become the famous Parliamentarian hero during the English Civil War. Sir Thomas fought at a number of the decisive battles of the war such as Marston Moor and Naseby. His reputation as a leader and a courageous warrior had grown so much that by January 1645 Parliament elected him lord-general of the New Model Army. During the Civil War he was to receive a number of wounds, some quite serious and life threatening. Although he was to recover from these, they would have a serious long-term effect on his general health, and from time to time he was to suffer from various other ailments such as rheumatism, kidney stones and gout. He never allowed his infirmities to prevent him from fighting; however, he did use them to excuse himself from participating in the difficult political machinations that

followed the king's defeat, as he was out of his depth in political intrigue. After the Restoration of the Monarchy in 1660, Sir Thomas retired from public life and lived quietly in Yorkshire until his death in 1671.

Denton Hall remained the property of the Fairfax family until it was sold by the wife of the fifth Lord Fairfax in around 1700 to Henry Ibbetson of Leeds. The Ibbetson family were exceedingly skilled farmers and famous for breeding shorthorn cattle. Although they actively improved the estate, they were to suffer much misfortune, and in around 1734 the original building burnt down. The hall was rebuilt by Samuel Ibbetson, only to be burnt down once more, nine years after the first fire. The building we can see today was designed by John Carr of York, who was also responsible for Harewood House. He had been commissioned by Sir John Ibbetson at a total cost of £100,000. The years that followed brought a change of ownership in 1845, 1920, 1925 and finally 1976. Today, Denton Hall is a venue for corporate events and weddings and is set in 2,500 acres of stunning Yorkshire countryside, with breathtaking panoramas of Ilkley, the moor and the River Wharfe.

THOMAS CHIPPENDALE

Born in Otley in 1718, the son of a carpenter, Thomas Chippendale's name was to become synonymous with fine English furniture. He was a contemporary of Robert Adams, the famous British architect. Little is known about his early life before he moved to London in 1749, where he became the first cabinetmaker to publish a book of designs. It is perhaps for his furniture that Thomas Chippendale is remembered most, although he was much more than just a cabinetmaker. He was also an interior designer who advised on soft furnishings and colour schemes. Examples of his furniture can be seen at Harewood House and Nostell Priory, which is reputed to have the finest collection of Chippendale's work in the world.

Statue of Thomas Chippendale, Otley.

FARNLEY HALL

Farnley Hall was first built in Elizabethan times by Sir Thomas Danby, whose great-great grandson, also called Thomas, was to become the first Lord Mayor of Leeds. In 1985 an archaeological survey discovered evidence of a mediaeval deer park, and this is supported by Farnley being mentioned in the *Domesday Book*. Farnley Hall is located south-west of Leeds and is not to be mistaken with the other Farnley Hall, which is in North Yorkshire and was the home of the Fawkes family.

Very little of the original building remains, as the hall was partially demolished and rebuilt in the mid-18th century. To the rear of the building remains the original inscription, albeit much eroded, stating the year of the hall's construction and that it had been built by Sir Thomas Danby. In 1799 the hall was sold to James Armitage, a Leeds wool merchant. The hall and grounds were purchased by Leeds City Council in 1945 and now make up Farnley Hall Park, which covers five acres consisting of formal gardens, shrubberies and woodland. There is also a fish pond that was created shortly after the Napoleonic wars as a scheme to create work for the unemployed.

BRAMHOPE TUNNEL

In the churchyard of Otley Parish Church stands a memorial to the 23 men who lost their lives constructing the Bramhope Tunnel. It had been the brainchild of a number of businessmen, who in 1843 published plans to produce a rail link between Thirsk and Leeds. It was estimated that the whole enterprise would cost £800,000 to complete. Despite opposition to the plan, approval was granted by Parliament in 1845, and by October of that year work had begun on the tunnel, which would eventually take four years to complete. The final cost was to escalate to £2,150,313. The project had been given to a certain James Bray, who was an iron and brass founder from Leeds. He certainly was not a novice, for this was not his first tunnel as he had already successfully completed the Thackley Tunnel near Bradford.

The building of the tunnel was hard and dangerous work. As well as dealing with the hard rock, which was difficult to tunnel through, there was the constant threat of flooding. It has been calculated that a staggering billion and a half gallons of water was pumped

The memorial to those who lost their lives in making the Bramhope tunnel.

out during the construction. This first task was to sink an airshaft, and in total 20 shafts were eventually sunk (only four still remain – the others have since been filled in). The actual tunnelling operation started when James Bray laid the first stone in July 1846.

Although airshafts had been sunk, the ventilation was still poor and the air would have been foul and acrid from the fumes of gunpowder. Apart from the danger of flooding, there was always the possibility of the roof collapsing. The conditions for the navvies who worked on this enterprise were harsh and backbreaking. Each navvy could clear up to 20 tonnes of rock during a single shift, which would last 12 hours, often for seven days a week. For this, though, they were paid above average wages at 30 shillings a week (£1.50) compared with a farm labourer who might receive 10 shillings (50p) and a hand-loom weaver who, although regarded as semi-skilled, could only expect five shillings and six-pence (approximately 27p). The navvies' reputation was without doubt awesome compared to the average labourer; with his super-human strength and his gargantuan appetites in food, drink and fighting, he was a force to be reckoned with. It was normal for the navvy to consume two pounds of meat, two pounds of bread and five quarts of ale a day, and there were stories of navvies being permanently inebriated.

Bramhope Tunnel is two miles and 243 yards long, 25ft 6in wide and 25ft high. It travels from Horsforth to Arthington and at its deepest point is about 290ft below the surface. The southern entrance to the tunnel is plain and ordinary; however, the northern entrance is a fabulous model of a castle that is hidden by woods and embankment (the memorial at Otley is a replica of the northern entrance). On 31 May 1849, when the first train travelled through the tunnel, it was the contractor's own locomotive called *Stephenson* and it carried officials from the railway company. A month later the official 'grand' opening took place.

CALVERLEY

In 1605 an anonymous pamphlet was published with the title of 'Two most unnaturall and bloodie murthers: the one by Maister Caverley [sic], a Yorkshire gentleman, practised upon his wife, and committed upon his two children, the three and twentie of Aprill 1605', which tells the tale of Sir Walter Calverley and his heinous crime. The pamphlet tells us that Master Walter Calverley, although orphaned and made ward of a guardian, had been left an ample inheritance and one that should have offered him a comfortable and secure future. He became betrothed to the daughter of a local gentleman before moving to London where, forgetting his promise, he marries another. When his first betrothed hears of this she becomes sick with grief. Despite her grief, she is of such a gentle disposition that she forgives his betrayal and wishes them both 'prosperous health and fruitful wealth'.

It was his taste in riotous living that was to prove his ultimate downfall, and before long he had found it necessary to mortgage his land as he ran up great debts. With mounting money worries, he became sullen and moody, and when his wife inquired as to what was the cause of his sadness, he cursed her with the words, 'A plague on thee! Thou art the cause of my sadness'. With her husband demanding money from her, she went to London to sell her dowry, but instead of doing so she secured promise of employment for her husband from his former guardian; however, during her absence his habits had grown worse, and he was given to excess of rioting, gambling, drinking and revelling. His mood became black, and he was unable to contain his rage, proclaiming his wife a 'strumpet' and his three sons illegitimate. His allegations fell on the ears of a gentleman who had known his wife since

Calverley Hall.

birth and, intending to protect her reputation, the two soon fell into a quarrel that culminated in the fighting of a duel. During the fight Master Calverley was wounded and at the gentleman's mercy, but his life was spared by the gentleman, who had no wish to take it as he felt that there was good in him and he could yet redeem his good name. But Master Calverley saw his wounds as the fault of his wife and, looking for revenge for his humiliation, he had decided to make his wife pay.

On her return he learnt that she had failed to sell her dowry, and when he discovered that she had secured employment for him with his former guardian he became white with rage and accused her of spreading tales about him in London. The pamphlet goes on to tell that a stranger brought him news that his brother had been committed to prison due to his debts. At that moment he began to see his world falling apart, the ruination of his ancient house and the loss of his family reputation, which once was the best in Yorkshire. It was at that moment when his torment was at its greatest when his eldest son, the four-year-old William walked in

on his father and asked, 'How do you do, Father?' In a fit of rage Walter Calverley lifted up his son by the neck and plunged his dagger into him. Holding the wounded child at arm's length to keep the blood from his clothes he carried him to the chamber where his wife slept. As he entered the chamber a servant woman, seeing his murderous intent, attempted to protect mother and child, but he flung her aside down a flight of steps. The commotion awoke his wife, who swept up the youngest child in her arms to protect it. Unable to wrench the child away, he killed it in her arms and stabbed her, a number of times. The dagger only penetrated her once, as the whale-bones in her corset deflected the blows. She fell to the floor, still clutching her dead child, but fortunately she was to survive her wounds.

The noise had alerted other servants who, finding the woman servant lying at the bottom of the stairs and under the impression that she had slipped, began to see to her needs when the young William, who was weak from the loss of blood, staggered to the top of the stairs. The child fell down the steps dead at the feet of the

Thornhill Arms, Calverley.

though he had done no wrong. At a subsequent trial he refused to make a plea or answer their charges, and on 5 August 1605 he was 'pressed to death' by placing heavy stones on him in an attempt to make him talk, but he remained silent and died.

It appears that the tale captured the imagination of the population to such an extent that, as well as the published pamphlet, there was also a play produced telling of the crime. Calverley Old Hall still stands, although it was divided into cottages in the 17th century when the Calverley family sold their land and property to the Thornhills and moved to Esholt. It was due to the conversion to cottages that the hall was saved from any form of Victorian or Edwardian modernisation. The oldest part of the building dates from around 1380 and was originally a timber frame, which was to be later encased in stone. On the main road through Calverley stands the village's oldest pub, once called The Leopard but now known as the Thornhill Arms. Inside the public house can be found a stone with the inscription '1673 WC' – the WC standing for Walter Calverley.

shocked servants. Two of his sons lay dead, but a third was with a nurse 12 miles away. Master Calverley, taking a horse from his stable, rode with the intention of despatching this third child, but as he grew close to his destination his horse collapsed on top of him, and those who were in pursuit were able to capture him. His captors took him to Sir John Saville's, from where he was then taken to Wakefield prison. The journey took him past his own home, and he begged them to allow him to see his wife. Strange as it may seem, she kissed him as

Calverley Cutting.

*St Wilfred's
Church,
Calverley.*

In 1856 the Thornhill family created 'Calverley Cutting' as a route from Calverley through to Apperley Bridge. This was to replace the ancient packhorse track that wound its way through the woods. The Thornhills had planned to build some superior villas on its site, although they faced strong objections at a public meeting. The critics said that the cutting was too steep for 'a weakly person to ascend' and that it was not as picturesque as the old winding path through the woods.

PUDSEY

For many centuries Pudsey was part of the ancient parish of Calverley although they had separate histories going back at least a millenium, with Pudsey soon becoming the richer of the two townships. In the *Domesday Book*, Pudsey or Podeschesaie as it was then referred to had, before the Normans laid it to waste, land worth 40 shillings, whereas Calverley was only worth 20 shillings. It was not until 1878, however, that

Pudsey became a parish in its own right. The church that was to become the parish church had been built 57 years earlier and had been the idea of Reverend David Jenkins, who initially applied for a grant to build a new church under the 1818 Church Building Act. The act was also known as the 'Million Act' because the government had provided £1,000,000 to build new churches, and this was increased by another £500,000 a few years

*St Lawrence's
Church, Pudsey.*

41

later when Austria unexpectedly paid off a war loan, giving the government a sudden windfall.

David Jenkins laid the first stone in 1821 for the Church of St Lawrence as the new church was to be called. Unusually, the church was to have a roof of Westmorland slate instead of using local stone, and this would have added to the expense of what was already an expensive building. During the building work, one of the slaters tragically lost his life falling from the roof, and the headstone of the unfortunate John Johnson from Bowness can be found in the churchyard. It was consecrated on 30 August 1824 by the Archbishop of York, who led a procession up the aisle quoting the 24th Psalm – *The Earth is the Lord's.*

As with many of its neighbours, Pudsey shares the age-old tradition of cloth manufacturing and during the 19th century enjoyed relative economic success. This success is reflected in the growth of the population of the township, which increased almost nine-fold in a little over a century. In 1900 Pudsey was granted a Charter of Incorporation, which entitled it to a mayor and a corporation; however, following the local government reorganisation of 1974, the borough of Pudsey became part of the Leeds Metropolitan District. Although there were many mills and much industry throughout the district, there can still be found large areas of unspoilt countryside and woodlands. Even today there is still an abundance of industry in and around Pudsey, but despite this there are many pleasant country walks and ancient rights of way to explore.

FULNECK MORAVIAN VILLAGE

Set on hillside overlooking a deep valley, through which Pudsey Beck flows, is the

The opening of a public park was once a momentous occasion, and it was no different for Pudsey Park when opened in October 1889. The festivities were spectacular, starting with a procession led by two brass bands and culminating in the evening with illuminations and the best firework display that Pudsey had ever seen. The park gates were opened with a solid silver key, which had been specially made for the grand celebration. The crowds were so great that the speeches were forced to be cut short. Today Pudsey Park is still a pleasant place for the family to spend some time.

picturesque Fulneck Moravian settlement. Founded in 1744, it was named after a town in Northern Moravia in the Czech Republic called Fulnek. The settlers were members of the Moravian Church and descendants of the Czech Unity of Brethren. It was not long after making Fulneck their home that they had built a chapel, housing and a school. Initially it was a separate boys' and girls' school, but the two amalgamated in 1994.

The 'Father of American Architecture', Benjamin Henry Boneval Latrobe, was born on 1 May 1764 at the Fulneck Moravian Settlement. His American mother had originally been sent to the Moravian school at Fulneck by her father. His father had been responsible for all the Moravian schools in Britain. At the age of 12 Benjamin was sent to a seminary at Niesky in Silesia on the borders of Saxony and Poland. Four years later, while travelling through Germany, he joined the

A Moravian church at Fulneck village, Pudsey.

A row of cottages at Fulneck village, Pudsey.

The birthplace of Benjamin Latrobe.

Prussian army. It was during his time with the army that he was to become close friends with an officer from the American army. He eventually left the army when he was badly injured, and while recovering from his injuries he undertook the Grand Tour. Through his education and travels he became fluent in a number of languages, including German, French, Greek and Latin.

After returning to England in 1784, he became apprenticed to the engineer John Smeaton, who had built the Eddystone Lighthouse. A short time later he was to take up another apprenticeship, this time with Samuel Pepys Cockerall, eminent architect and great-great nephew of the famous diarist (Samuel Pepys). It was not long, however, before Benjamin was in practice for himself and had completed a number of projects. In 1790 he married Lydie Sellon, although sadly the marriage was short-lived as she died three years later. They had two children together. She had inherited her father's wealth, which in turn had been left to her children in a trust that their uncle controlled. Unfortunately the children were swindled by their uncle and never saw a penny of it. After the death of his wife, events took a turn for the worse and culminated in him losing custody of his children and being declared bankrupt. In 1795 he set off for America. The journey took four months, and

Latrobe eventually arrived in Norfolk, Virginia, on 20 March 1796.

It was not long before he was building a reputation for himself. While journeying throughout Europe he had collected many ideas and had developed his principles for urban planning for designing and locating American cities. He was extremely concerned about public health, and due to the way the wind blows he believed that it was much healthier to build on the western banks of rivers. He was to complete many projects throughout the country, but perhaps his greatest achievement was as the designer of the American Capitol and notably the White House. He was to eventually die in 1820 from yellow fever while working on a waterworks project in New Orleans.

THE FARNLEY WOOD PLOT

Barely a footnote in West Yorkshire's history, the Northern Risings of 1663, following the Restoration of the Monarchy, have gone largely unnoticed. Like most rebellions that have floundered before they have really begun, they have been dismissed as having very little historical significance. But, however insignificant this rebellion may seem, it ended with the execution of 26 men, 16 of whom met their end by the most gruesome method imaginable: being hung, drawn and quartered.

The objective of the Farnley Wood plot was to capture and overthrow the Royalist strongholds in Leeds. The two main characters and ringleaders in this plot were Joshua Greathead and Captain Oates of Morley. Joshua was a local squire and had fought with the Parliamentarians during the Civil War and was the leader of his own squadron. Captain Thomas Oates, who was a cousin of Joshua, had also fought on the side of the Roundheads. The plan had been for a band of men to meet at Farnley on the morning of 12 October 1663, before heading off to storm Leeds. Their action would have almost certainly ended in a battle and bloodshed. Many of their number were farmers and local businessmen who really did not have much of a stomach for a fight. Also, there had been a poor turnout, with only 26 men eventually showing up. It was decided that the plot had been a failure and, disbanding, they headed home.

They had mistakenly thought that the authorities were oblivious to their plans, but they had been betrayed. Joshua Greathead had disagreed with the timing of the rebellion but had been overruled by Oates and the other men. He had then contacted the authorities and relayed every detail of their plans. The authorities did not act immediately but allowed Joshua to act as a spy and report back to them after each meeting. He alerted the authorities on the day when the group disbanded and the die was cast – all of the 26 were arrested.

All of the men were taken to York to stand trial for treason at the winter assizes. Three of the arrested men managed to escape, and they made their way back to Leeds, where they hid at an inn. It was not long, however, before they were in custody again, and on 14 January 1664 they were condemned to death for treason. They were taken to Chapeltown Moor, and the three men were hung, drawn and quartered before what is believed the largest crowd ever to gather in Leeds to watch an execution. It is interesting to note that it was only men who could expect this fate for high treason; women on the other hand were burnt at the stake. After the execution of the three men, the executioner, Peter Mason, took the three heads and parboiled them to preserve them. The heads were then mounted on the railings of the Moot Hall, and there they stayed until 1677 when the skulls blew down in a gale.

ADEL CHURCH

Widely considered to be one of the best remaining examples of Norman architecture, St John the Baptist's Church at Adel is a Grade I

The stunning Norman church at Adel.

listed 12th-century building with many outstanding features. Perhaps one of its best-known features is the elaborately carved stone doorway and the bronze Sanctuary Ring, which was cast in York in 1200. There is an interesting story concerning the Sanctuary Ring. If a couple

Church doorway, Adel.

Sanctuary Ring, Adel.

were too poor to buy a wedding ring they could be married in the church porch. Grasping the Sanctuary Ring, they would announce 'with this ring I thee wed'. Originally the church had a large stone porch, but it was removed in 1816. Sadly, this has caused the stonework to deteriorate, as it is open to the elements.

The word Adel comes from the Anglo-Saxon word 'adela' meaning a muddy or boggy place. It is believed that there had been a church at this site prior to this church, as there is an 11th-century charter that refers to the Church of St John of Adela. At one time the parish of Adel stretched over a considerable area, but this has diminished over the years. The church is located near the site of the Roman fort of Burgodunum, which was built on the ancient route from Ilkley to York. Two stone coffins that date from Norman times can be found at the gate of the church, as well as some Roman and Saxon stones. In 1926 Adel was merged into Borough of Leeds.

HAREWOOD HOUSE

Walking along the terrace of Harewood House, one cannot fail but to be impressed by the grandeur of this beautiful building. Built in 1771, Harewood House was the home of the Lascelles, who had purchased the estate after making their fortune in the West Indies. The house was designed by John Carr and Robert Adam, while much of the furniture was by Thomas Chippendale, who had been born locally at Otley.

Harewood House in the morning mist.

The grounds were the work of Lancelot 'Capability' Brown, the famous English landscape gardener responsible for many of the gardens and parks belonging to the grand homes of England. Harewood House and its estate were constructed almost virtually on the site of Gawthorpe, which had long been the home of the Gascoignes.

William Gascoigne was Lord Chief Justice of England in 1401. It is said that he was probably the most upright judge that ever lived in England. There is an interesting story that, although never corroborated, has been immortalised by the pen of William Shakespeare. A number of young men had been brought before the judge accused of a breach of the peace. Among the rowdy revellers was the future King Henry V. The judge, sickened by the violent deeds and ill-conduct of these men, committed most of them to prison when the prince strode up and struck Gascoigne in the face, which resulted in the prince also being committed to prison. Years later, when Henry was at his coronation in 1413, he paused before Gascoigne and said, 'You are assured, I think, that I love you not.' To which the old man replied, 'I am assured that if I be measured rightly, your Majesty hath no cause to hate me.' The King was furious at what he perceived to be an outrageous indignity, which he had been made to suffer by his period of incarceration. The old judge explained that it was the majesty, power of law and justice that he had represented, and it was by the authority of the king that he had acted. He went on to say that if one day the king should have a son who had no regard for his laws, he should be happy if he was able to rely on such as he to administer justice. The king, recognising the truth, agreed that he was happy to have such a bold and upright man to deliver his justice and maintain his laws. Judge Gascoigne is buried beneath a splendid monument in Harewood church.

Harewood House is still the home of the Lascelles family and the seat of the earls of Harewood. The present and seventh earl is George Henry Hubert Lascelles, the eldest son

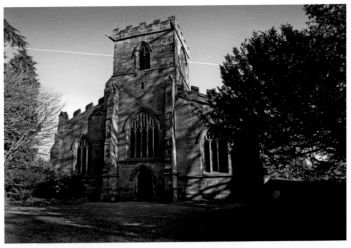

Church at Harewood.

of the sixth earl and Mary, Princess Royal. He is first cousin to the Queen and 42nd in line to the throne. The estate is owned and managed by the Harewood House Trust and is open to the public throughout most of the year. It won a Large Visitor Attraction of the Year award in 2003 and remains one of West Yorkshire's most popular places to visit.

WETHERBY

Originally the town of Wetherby, which lies midway between London and Edinburgh, was a staging post situated on the banks of the River Wharfe. Spanning the river is a stone bridge. The bridge is Wetherby's only designated 'Ancient Monument' and, although originally built in about 1233, it developed over the years into the impressive stone structure that we see today. A brief glance under one of the arches shows that the bridge has been widened, as the original structure is still clearly visible. When first built, the bridge was only 11ft wide, and it had been constructed with funds raised by Walter De Gray, the Archbishop of York. According to a plaque attached to the bridge, he raised the money from repenting sinners who paid to have their sins forgiven.

Wetherby's importance as a staging post can be seen from the number of coaching inns found along the main thoroughfare: The Swan and Talbot Inn, which had probably once been

Far right: The Swan & Talbot, a coaching house.

Wetherby Bridge arch, showing how it has been extended.

a monastic lodging house (or resting place for clerics); The Angel Inn, which has sometimes been known as the 'Halfway House' as it stood halfway between London and Edinburgh, and the Brunswick Arms. Between the years of 1760 and 1840, The Angel Inn was extremely important as a coaching inn as it provided stabling for over a hundred horses, and in addition it had its own smithy and farriers. In 1837 the inn received two mail coaches daily between London and Glasgow and between Manchester and Hull. Further up the road stands the Brunswick Arms and Brunswick Court, which was built in 1824. The court comprised of a posting horse stable (the Royal Mail) for eight horses. There was also stabling for another six horses, standing room for two coaches, granaries and hay lofts. Sadly, the arrival of the railways killed off this important source of the town's wealth.

Although only the foundations remain, there once stood a castle in Wetherby. It had been constructed by the Percy family during the civil

Wheel and Wetherby bridge.

Far left: A plaque that is attached to the side of Wetherby Town Hall, commemorating the granting of the right to hold a weekly market by Henry III to the Knights Templar.

The Little Nipper: the mousetrap invented by James Henry Atkinson, still proves to be one of the most effective traps on the market.

wars that followed the death of Henry I and had been built to protect the river crossing from the Scottish armies that controlled the northern counties of England, including North Yorkshire at that time. Unfortunately the castle was built without royal permission, and Henry II ordered it to be demolished (it is pity that they could not have got retrospective planning permission).

Over time Wetherby developed into a busy market town, and on 15 November 1240 Henry III granted a charter for the Brethren of the Knighthood of the Temple of Solomon (the Knights Templar) to hold a Thursday market each week. It is interesting to note that Wetherby, or Werreby as it was known in the charter, still holds its market on a Thursday.

BOSTON SPA

Originally called Thorp Spa, the town of Boston Spa was established in 1744 when a certain John Shires discovered magnesium, limestone and sulphur springs in the area. Its popularity as a spa town was to decline when Harrogate became popular. However, for a while its popularity was such that in 1753 Joseph Tait was prompted to build the Royal Hotel to accommodate the visitors to the spa. The hotel is still standing, but it has now been converted into shops and flats. In the early 19th century a spa baths was built to allow visitors to enjoy the waters, and although the town had a population of around only 600 it had several inns and other properties offering accommodation.

JAMES HENRY ATKINSON

James Henry Atkinson (1849–1942) was an inventor and ironmonger from Leeds. Probably his most well-known invention was the mousetrap called the 'Little Nipper'. He was to make his first prototype in 1897 and eventually patented his idea in 1910. This simple device has never been bettered and still enjoys a 60 per cent share of the market throughout the world. Simple it may be, but there is no denying its effectiveness: a spring trap that slams shut at a speed of 38,000th of a second (a record that has never been beaten). James sold his patent to Procter Bros Ltd in 1913 for £1,000, and they are still manufacturing them to this day.

TEMPLE NEWSAM

The history of Temple Newsam goes back to at least the 11th century, when it is recorded in the *Domesday Book* as the Manor of Newsam. In the 12th century it became the property of the Knights Templar, and it was during excavations carried out in 1991 that a farmstead belonging to the Knights was discovered a little further south of the present house and nearer to the River Aire. It is called Temple Newsam as a reference to the

Knights. After the Knights were disbanded in 1312, on the orders of Pope Clement V, the estate passed to the Darcy family. It was Thomas Lord Darcy who was to build the first house in around 1500, but sadly only the west wing remains of what was once a marvellous four-sided house around a courtyard. A crony of Cardinal Wolsey, Thomas was a courtier and mercenary who was beheaded for his part in the 'Pilgrimage of Grace'. His estates were forfeited, and Temple Newsam was given to the Countess of Lennox by Henry VIII.

It was at Temple Newsam that the Countess of Lennox gave birth to her two sons Lord Charles Stuart and the infamous Henry Lord Darnley, who eventually married Mary, Queen of Scots when he was just 19. Born in 1545, he was a descendant of a daughter of James II of Scotland, which placed him in line for the throne of Scotland. Darnley was a petty and violent man and was not popular with the other nobles. Together with a group of his supporters, he murdered Mary's private secretary, David Rizzio, in the presence of the queen. This bloody murder took place at Holyrood Palace. He was to meet his end on 10 February 1567 while staying in Edinburgh, escaping one attempt on his life by fleeing the house he was staying in, only to be murdered in the garden.

When Queen Elizabeth I came to the throne she confiscated Temple Newsam and threw the Countess of Lennox into the Tower of London. The property was now the property of the Crown. This was followed by almost 80 years of neglect, until in 1622 the property was bought for £12,000 by Sir Arthur Ingram. Sir Arthur was a courtier and an entrepreneur who, having amassed his great wealth in London, decided to move back to his native Yorkshire. The house was to see a great deal of change, as he demolished three sides of the Tudor house to rebuild it with two new wings. In 1628 he completed the work and added the inscription: 'ALL GLORY AND PRAISE BE GIVEN TO GOD THE FATHER THE SON AND THE HOLY GHOST ON HIGH PEACE ON EARTH GOOD WILL TOWARDS MEN HONOUR AND TRUE ALLEGIANCE TO OUR GRACIOUS KING LOVING AFFECTION AMONGST HIS SUBJECTS HEALTH AND PLENTY BE WITHIN THIS HOUSE', which was to be said as a daily prayer by the assembled household in the chapel.

The English Civil War was to see a great divide in the family as his sons took opposite sides in the conflict. Sir Arthur's grandson Henry joined the exiled court and was rewarded for his loyalty with the title of Viscount Irwin at the Restoration of the Monarchy. Sadly, both Henry and his wife were extremely extravagant, and after his untimely death in 1666 many of the house furnishings had to be sold off. A period of prosperity was to follow when the third viscount, Arthur, inherited the property in 1688. His wife Isabella Machell had brought with her as part of the marriage settlement two parliamentary seats, which guaranteed the family a powerful position. After his death in 1702, she kept a tight control of family affairs until her death at the ripe old age of 94.

In the mid-18th century the house was remodelled and new bedrooms added, but perhaps the most impressive feature was that the north wing had been turned into an art gallery with a library attached. In 1760 the famous Capability Brown had been employed to re-landscape the grounds. Much work was done to the house in the late 19th century to restore its Tudor and Jacobean grandeur. This work was carried out by the widow of the last Ingram to own the property, Hugo Charles Meynell Ingram who had died prematurely. Mrs Meynell Ingram lived at the house for another 33 years until her death in 1904. The couple had been childless, and therefore on her death she left the property to her nephew, Edward Fredrick Lindley Wood, the first Earl of Halifax. He sold the property, including the park, to Leeds Corporation on the condition that their preservation was ensured for the future.

Fairburn Ings.

It is said that the house is the most haunted place in Yorkshire. Today the house and park is open to the public and is the venue for many leisure activities, including horseriding, golf and cycling to name but a few. It was also the site of the Leeds Festival between 1999 until 2002, but sadly the venue has been forced to move due to violence and riots on the grounds of this grand old estate. Temple Newsam has had a colourful and perhaps chequered past, but it well deserves its reputation as one of the great historic estates of England.

FAIRBURN INGS

Since being declared a Local Nature Reserve in 1957, Fairburn Ings has been regarded as a site of national importance for wildfowl. The reserve is managed by the Royal Society for the Protection of Birds on the behalf of Leeds City Council. With an area covering 286 hectares of land, it is on record that the reserve has the highest number of bird species of any nature reserve in England. Due to its location, it is regularly flooded by the River Aire (Ings is of Old Norse origin meaning 'damp or marshy land'). There is a large lake and a number of smaller bodies of water, all of which have been the result of subsidence caused by former coal mining, with some tunnels running up to half a kilometre beneath the surface. A good proportion of the reserve has been landscaped from 26 million cubic metres of colliery spoil, which has been used to create a large area of rich grassland, wetland and woodland.

Not only is the reserve a delight for the dedicated ornithologist, it also has much to offer the casual walker looking for somewhere to enjoy a pleasant stroll in an area of outstanding beauty.

THE CITY OF BRADFORD

The origins of Bradford as an Anglo-Saxon settlement are obscure, but in all probability it was so named on account of the fact that it was started at the site of a 'broad ford' over Bradford Beck - 'brad' being the Anglo-Saxon word for 'broad'. This settlement grew in size, and by the 11th century it consisted of approximately 350 people, which was quite large by the standards of the day. During the 'Harrying of the North' by William the Conqueror, however, Bradford shared the fate of many of its neighbours and was laid to waste. It possessed no church, parish, castle or manor house and had to rely on Dewsbury for its ecclesiastical and spiritual needs and Pontefract for its civil needs. Certainly, by 1316 it is clear that a cloth industry of sorts had commenced, as there is evidence of the existence of a fulling-mill. Over the next 200 years the city saw an improvement in its prosperity, and by the Middle Ages Bradford not only had a thriving woollen industry, but it was also a centre for leather tanning. It is not surprising that, given the number of sheep in West Yorkshire, the region would also have a large tannery industry. In 1461 Bradford was granted the right to hold two fairs a year, just like its neighbour Leeds, and this would have been important for the city, for these lucrative fairs would have generated much wealth.

Bradford's coat of arms includes a boar's head and three hunting horns, which, according to legend, was adopted because of an event that took place during the Middle Ages. The inhabitants of Bradford had been terrorised by a large and vicious boar that was roaming the lands. The lord of the manor had offered a reward to anyone who could kill the beast and rid the people of Bradford of this menace. It is said that John Rushworth saw the boar drinking at a well and, catching the ferocious beast unawares, he killed it. Removing the tongue as proof, he started off to see the lord. Unfortunately before he could get there another hunter came upon the dead boar and cut off its head. Somehow this second man managed to reach the lord first, but it was discovered that the tongue was missing. He was unable to offer an explanation, at which point John Rushworth arrived with the missing tongue, and he earned his reward of a plot of land, which to this day is still called Hunt Yard.

Over the centuries the fortunes of Bradford fluctuated, for it suffered greatly during the outbreaks of plague and throughout the English Civil War. In spite of its many misfortunes Bradford's woollen industry continued to grow. There was surge in growth in the 17th century when the people of Bradford began to concentrate on worsted instead of woollen cloth. But it was not until the late 18th century that Bradford witnessed incredible growth. In 1780 the city had a

Opposite: The Granddad's Clock & Chair: a sculpture by Timothy Shutter represents a mill owner's office, and although it is looking to the past the swinging pendulum is intended to remind us that time does not stand still.

Fibres – a contemporary sculpture by Ian Randall. It represents the regeneration of this former railway site and is located in St Blaise Court. St Blaise was the patron saint of woolcombing.

population of 4,500, and in little over 70 years it had exploded to over 100,000. The Industrial Revolution had begun and Bradford was ready to take full advantage. Bradford was to see rapid progress and change at a tremendous rate, and today as we travel around this wonderful city it is impossible not to admire the legacy that our ancestors left.

BRADFORD CATHEDRAL

Bradford Cathedral is situated on Church Bank and overlooks what was once the original 'broad ford' over Bradford Beck from which Bradford took its name. The ford no longer exists as the beck now travels beneath the city centre. Sadly, over much of the 20th century the cathedral has been hidden away behind other buildings, and it has been easy to forget that Bradford possesses such a lovely historical church; however, many buildings have been pulled down to make room for new developments, which has meant that once again the cathedral is a visible landmark in Bradford.

The cathedral has a long and illustrious history, which stretches back to 627 when Paulinus, on a mission to Northumbria,

Bradford Cathedral.

preached at Dewsbury. It was from there that Bradford was evangelised. At the time of the *Domesday Book* it would have been highly likely that there was some sort of church at the site of where the present cathedral stands, as it would have been inconceivable for there not to be a place of worship for the lord of the manor to attend, even if it was, at the very least, some wooden structure.

In the register of the Archbishop of York it was recorded in 1281 that Alice de Lacy, widow of one of Ilbert's descendants, gave a grant to the Parish of Bradford. It is known that there was a stone church at the site by the early 14th century, as it was burnt down in the year 1327. This act of arson was possibly carried out by Scottish raiders. Around this time the church was rebuilt, and it is probable that some of the older stonework was used in the new construction. As with many churches, it suffered much damage during the Reformation of the mid-16th century. During the English Civil War Bradford was a Parliamentary stronghold and was under siege in 1642 and again in 1643. Woolsacks were hung from the church tower in an attempt to protect it from

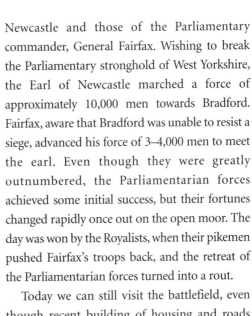

State stairs at Bradford Cathedral.

the Royalist cannons. There are a number of sketches that survive from the period showing this to be the case. These are thought to be the work of some trooper, who may have possibly done them to while away an idle moment during a lull in the fighting.

Even though as late as the 18th century the parish church was Bradford's only church, it was to witness many changes to its fortunes as many were turning away from the Anglican Church in favour of the dissenters, such as the Methodists. In the 19th century new parishes were formed within the original parish; however, this building was to retain its status as the parish church of Bradford. In 1919 it became a cathedral when the Diocese of Bradford was created. During the 1950s and 1960s the building was extended by the local architect Sir Edward Brantwood Maufe, who was born in 1883 in Ilkley.

THE BATTLE OF ADWALTON MOOR

On 30 June 1643 the Battle of Adwalton Moor took place high above Bradford. The battle was between the Royalist forces of the Earl of Newcastle and those of the Parliamentary commander, General Fairfax. Wishing to break the Parliamentary stronghold of West Yorkshire, the Earl of Newcastle marched a force of approximately 10,000 men towards Bradford. Fairfax, aware that Bradford was unable to resist a siege, advanced his force of 3–4,000 men to meet the earl. Even though they were greatly outnumbered, the Parliamentarian forces achieved some initial success, but their fortunes changed rapidly once out on the open moor. The day was won by the Royalists, when their pikemen pushed Fairfax's troops back, and the retreat of the Parliamentarian forces turned into a rout.

Today we can still visit the battlefield, even though recent building of housing and roads has led to a dramatic change to many parts of the site. It has fortunately managed to retain several of its features, which would have been visible on that day nearly four centuries ago.

ABRAHAM BALME

In the north wall of the chancel of Bradford Cathedral can be found a white marble tablet memorial to Abraham Balme. He was born in 1706 and was the eldest son of a farmer from Thornton. Living to the ripe old age of 90, he was to witness many significant changes to Bradford throughout his long life, as it changed from being a rural market town into one of the major players of the Industrial Revolution. He was to play an important role in these changes, and his interests were as diverse as wool, mining, banking and property. Not only was he to acquire a considerable estate at Bowling, which he worked tirelessly to increase, but eventually his personal estates included land in Tong, Horton, Birstall and Hopton. Bowling was especially important as it was rich in mineral deposits. Between the years of 1753 and 1766 he was to act as steward to the lord of the manor, Thomas Pigot. As well as leasing mines to others, Abraham organised Pigot's labourers and worked the mines on his behalf.

Bingley Five Rise Locks.

It was his involvement in mining that lead to his interest in seeking improved modes of transport, which in turn led to his interest in canals. He was heavily involved with the building of both the Leeds Liverpool and the Bradford canals. His interests did not stop at industry and commerce as he was a committed supporter of friendly societies, and he was also deeply involved with Bradford Parish. Although only one in a growing band of landowners who were to change the face of Bradford, the part he played was significant nonetheless.

RICHARD OASTLER

In the centre of Rawson Square in Bradford stands the statue of Richard Oastler, a remarkable man whose story deserves telling. Oastler was born on 20 December 1789 in St Peter's Square in Leeds. His father, called Robert, was originally a linen merchant from Thirsk and settled in Leeds before becoming steward for the Thornhills at the Fixby estates near Huddersfield. Robert Oastler had been disinherited by his father when he became a Methodist. During Richard's childhood John

Richard Oastler.

Wesley was to become a familiar figure to the young boy as he was a regular visitor to the Oastler household. It is said that on Wesley's last visit he took up the young Richard into his arms and blessed him. Richard was educated at the Fulneck Moravian School near Pudsey, Leeds, and his childhood ambition was to

become a barrister. His father had other ideas, though, and articled him to Charles Watson an architect in Wakefield. He only lasted four years in the profession as he was forced to leave due to poor eyesight.

Richard became a commission agent, and through hard work he accumulated a considerable wealth, only to lose everything in 1820. It was a tragic year for Richard as his father passed away in the July. Thomas Thornhill appointed him steward at an annual salary of £300, and Richard devoted himself to the role. He was already well-known in the region for his strong views and since 1807 had been an advocate for the abolition of slavery. As a dedicated Tory, who was also against Parliamentary reforms and Trade Unions, a less likely radical reformer was hard to imagine. He also believed in the rigid class structure of the early 19th century, which appears to make his tireless efforts to gain improvements in the working hours of children even more remarkable. During a business visit in 1830 to John Wood of Horton Hall (a worsted manufacturer from Bradford), Wood had grabbed Richard's hand and pressed it into his in an 'impressive manner' and said, 'I have had no sleep tonight. I have been reading the Bible and in every page I have read my own condemnation. I cannot allow you to leave me without a pledge that you will use all your influence in trying to remove from our factory system the cruelties which are practised in our mills.' Richard, although no doubt taken aback by this man's outburst, promised that he would do everything that he could to help.

A man of his word, on the very same day, Richard wrote a letter entitled *Yorkshire Slavery*, which he submitted to the *Leeds Mercury*. In the letter he described what he had heard, but its publication was met with denial and criticism. By establishing the truth of his statements he went on to gain the gratitude of all working men. From that moment on he worked tirelessly to obtain a reduction in their working hours. He arranged committees and addressed meetings, and in 1832 he organised a 'Pilgrimage of Mercy' to York. Nicknamed 'King' by his opponents; this was originally intended as a derogatory term, but it was a title that his friends were soon to use throughout Yorkshire and Lancashire as sign of their admiration. Oastler also took pleasure in using the title himself. After leaving the employment of Thomas Thornhill he was sued by his ex-employer for a debt of £2,000. Unable to pay, he was committed to the Fleet Prison. He was to stay incarcerated for the next three years until his friends could raise enough money to obtain his release. During his imprisonment he did not remain idle, but he published what he called *The Fleet Papers*. It was through these papers that he pleaded the cause of the factory workers, denounced the new Poor Law and defended the Corn Laws.

After his release from prison he continued to press for a 10-hour working day. The passing of Lord Ashley's Act effectively ended his public career. For a brief time in the 1850s he edited his own weekly newspaper called *The Home*, but after four years he discontinued it. Richard Oastler died in Harrogate on 22 August 1861 and was buried at Kirkstall.

Oastler had a commanding presence; a powerful man standing over 6ft tall. He was also a man with strong views and violent in his denunciations. His voice was described by Trollope as 'stentorian in its power and yet flexible, with a flow of language rapid and abundant'. As a tribute to this great man the nation paid for a statue by subscription. The greatest number of donations came from Bradford, so it was decided that it was here that the memorial should be sited. The figure was sculptured by John Biffile Philip and was cast in bronze, weighing 3 tonnes at a cost of £1,500. Another of the great reformers for the conditions of children, the Earl of Shaftsbury, fittingly unveiled the statue.

The front of St George's Hall.

ST GEORGE'S HALL

During a meeting between subscribers to the Bradford Infirmary and Alderman Samuel Smith in 1849, the idea of St George's Hall was put forward. To finance the project £10 shares were offered, and by the time the foundation stone was laid on 22 September 1851 they had raised £16,000. Designed in the Neo-Classical style by the firm of architects Lockwood and Mawson, the final cost of the building was £35,000, and it was officially opened by Queen Victoria and Prince Albert in 1853. The original seating capacity of this magnificent building was 3,500 but on some occasions it was known to hold as many as 5,000. St George's Hall remains a popular venue, although today its current capacity is less than 2,000.

Charles Dickens gave his first ever reading of *Bleak House* at St George's Hall in December 1854 and was to receive the fee of £100 for two nights in Bradford. He was later to write about his visit, saying that 'The hall is enormous and they expect to seat 3,700 people tonight. Notwithstanding which, it seems to me a tolerably easy place – except that the width of the platform is so very great to the eye at first.'

One of the carved heads on the side of St George's.

He was impressed with the building's acoustics and called it 'an easy place', by which it was assumed he meant it was easy to be heard clearly. Two years after Dickens's visit, an organ with 51 stops and 2,783 pipes was installed in the hall. The hall has entertained its audiences with famous acts and celebrities for over 150 years. Since 1865 it has been a regular venue of the Halle Orchestra. When Sir Charles Halle died suddenly in 1895, the orchestra played at St George's to an empty rostrum as a sign of respect. Conducting from his place, Brodsky, the orchestra leader, conducted the concert, opening with the *Dead March*.

Among other famous visitors to the hall was Winston Churchill, who in 1910 held a political rally there. The rally was interrupted by a group of Suffragettes, who had hidden under the stage and at an opportune moment during his speech leapt through a trapdoor and danced on the stage. Interestingly, Churchill was not opposed to women getting the vote, even though in 1906 when confronted by a woman bearing a banner he announced, 'Nothing would induce me to vote for giving women the franchise. I am not going

to be henpecked into a question of such importance'. In a Commons vote in 1917 he was to vote in favour of giving women the franchise.

St George's Hall has seen a number of changes through the years and has had to deal with some near tragedies, such as the fire in 1982 which caused £100,000 worth of damage. In 2003 it was closed for three months when cracks were discovered in the ceiling, but was re-opened in January 2004 with a performance by the Halle Orchestra. It is certainly a tribute to this grand old building that it still functions as a concert hall and provides a venue for such a variety of entertainment.

CARTWRIGHT HALL

Standing in Lister Park is one of Bradford's finest museums – Cartwright Hall. The hall was built as a memorial to Dr. Edmund Cartwright who had given Bradford so much. It was his invention of the power loom and the combing machine that had played such an important role in Bradford's growth and prosperity. The construction of a permanent tribute to this great man was the idea of the ageing Lord Masham. In 1898 he paid a visit to Manningham Park (now known as Lister Park) to visit the estate which had been his home from boyhood until early married life. He was dismayed to see the dilapidated state of the hall, which was then being used as a second-class restaurant. Lord Masham had sold the estate to Bradford Corporation in 1870 at a fraction of its true value. The sight of his former home in such a sad state deeply disturbed him and prompted him to write to the mayor, Thomas Speight, asking for a meeting to discuss its future. During the meeting Lord Masham offered £40,000 (the sum that Bradford Corporation had originally paid him for the estate). It was an offer that the corporation readily accepted.

Bradford Corporation suggested that the new hall should be a technological museum as this seemed to be a more fitting tribute to Cartwright. Ultimately it was decided that the Technical College, which had opened a number of years before, would probably be the more appropriate venue for scientific exhibitions. It

Cartwright Hall.

was consequently proposed to build Cartwright Hall as an art gallery and natural history museum. Lord Masham, keen to see progress on the proposal, immediately sent his promised donation to the mayor. The next stage was to employ the services of an architect. The usual practice in Bradford at that time was to request submissions in the form of a competition and choose the best design. In total they received 117 entries, which were judged by the renowned architect Alfred Waterhouse. The winning designers were John W. Simpson and E.J. Milner Allen of London. This proved to be a controversial decision, as it was normal for Bradford Corporation to employ only local firms. Although on the foundation stone the names of both partners appear, Mr Allen left the partnership soon after being awarded the contract, and Mr Simpson continued with the project alone. It was obvious that Mr Simpson had intended to impress, and the building was to prove to be a masterpiece.

Cartwright Hall would eventually cost far more than the original estimated £40,000, and Lord Masham graciously offered to cover half the costs of the increased expenditure and the council met the other half from its gas profits. Lord Masham laid the foundation stone on 24 May 1900, and it took four years to complete. It proved to be a difficult four years as they struggled against one delay after another. In 1901 there was the most violent rainfall ever recorded in Bradford, which flooded the foundations and caused the building work already done to collapse. It was then discovered that the subsoil was not suitable for the construction of the Hall and deeper foundations were needed. Apart from the elements, further delays were caused by workmen's strikes, and in total over a year's work was lost through industrial action. As a symbolic gesture, Lord Masham presented a great stone that had originally been used to form the engine bed at Lister's old mill. This was cut into four pieces and used as cornerstones for the foundations. Cartwright Memorial Hall was built on the prosperity of Manningham Mills. The hall was eventually opened by Lord Masham on 13 April 1904. He was accompanied by the mayor, the corporation

Far right: Monument to Sir Titus Salt in Lister Park, near the Norman Arch.

Statue of Lister.

Fossilised tree stump.

and many leading lights of the area. The ceremony was almost a disaster when the ornate key, specially designed by the architect for the occasion, had been misplaced. A plain key was fortunately found, and the ceremony went ahead as planned.

This stunning hall cannot fail to impress the visitor with its elegant grandeur from both the exterior and the interior. Baroque in style, or sometimes referred to as 'Bradford Baroque' due to the number of buildings in Bradford built in this manner, Cartwright Hall was and indeed still is fit for a lord. In front of the main entrance to the hall stands a life-sized bronze statue of the huntress Diana with a deer. Other statues that can be found in Lister Park are one of Lord Masham, which had been commissioned in 1875 by the people of Bradford as a token of their esteem, and also that of Sir Titus Salt, which originally stood outside the town hall but was placed in the park in 1896.

Only a few feet from Salt's monument stands the Norman Arch entrance, which had been constructed in the park in 1883 and designed by the architect Mr Frank Healy. It was a replica of a wood and canvas structure that had been erected to celebrate a visit by the Prince and Princess of Wales, Edward and Alexandra. Originally it was built like a true Norman Arch, with a large arch and a small arch by its side; however the city architect, a believer in symmetry, added another arch. In 1889 a fossilized tree stump and its roots, which are now exhibited in the park, were found at a nearby quarry at Clayton. Calculated to be 330 million years old, it grew in a forest during the Carboniferous period when Yorkshire would have been a hot, steamy swamp that lay near the equator. When alive, the tree would have been about 40 yards high. Cartwright Hall and Lister Park remain a monument to these great men and are lovingly cared-for places that are ideal to while away a pleasant few hours, either looking at the magnificent art within the hall or wandering around the park enjoying the fresh air.

BRADFORD CITY HALL

Queen Victoria signed the Charter of Incorporation in 1847, which united the townships of Bradford, Manningham, Bowling

City Hall, Bradford.

Detail of City Hall showing windows and statues.

and Horton and bestowed on them the status of a Borough. With the Charter came the permission to elect a mayor, 14 aldermen and 42 councillors. It was not, however, until 1869 that it was decided that a purpose-built town hall was required, as for the preceding 26 years council business had taken place in the Fire Station House, which was sited in Swaine Street. After the land was purchased to build the town hall it was decided to hold a competition to design the new civic building. Lockwood and Mawson, a local firm of architects beat off 31 other competitors to be awarded the contract and John Ives & Son of Shipley were employed as builders. This magnificent building was opened on 9 September 1873 by the mayor, Alderman Matthew Thompson at a total cost of £100,000.

The original building was 275ft long, 70ft high and had the bell tower standing 217ft. By the end of the 19th century it was decided that the building was too small and would have to be extended. In 1909 a new council chamber, committee rooms and a banqueting hall was

opened. This was followed five years later with the addition of a grand staircase and a redesigned entrance. In November 1965 the town hall changed its name to City Hall as it was thought that this would be more in keeping with Bradford's status as a city.

Among a number of interesting features found on the exterior of City Hall are the 35 statues of the rulers of England from William the Conqueror to Queen Victoria. It is also interesting to note that there is one statue among them who was not a monarch – Oliver Cromwell, Lord Protector. Although his third son Richard took

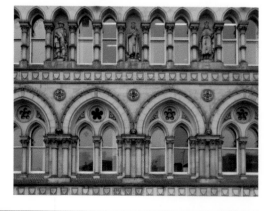

Henry V: one of the 35 statues on City Hall.

over the title of Lord Protector in 1658, after the death of Oliver, his statue does not appear. It is said that each statue is a faithful likeness, individually carved from local stone at a cost of £63 each. Apart from Queen Victoria and Queen Elizabeth I, who appear in a canopied niche on either side of the main entrance, all the other statues appear in chronological order.

Another feature of City Hall that should not be overlooked is its outstanding Italianate Clock Tower, soaring above the sky line, which was inspired by the Palazzo Vecchio in Florence. Within the tower are 13 bells that have a combined weight of 17 tonnes. The bells had lain silent since 1992 due to decay in the bell frame; however, with help from the National Lottery in 1997 the bells were able to ring once more. The bells chime every 15 minutes and play tunes at lunchtime and teatime. As a mark of respect for those who lost their lives in terrorist attacks of 9/11, the bells rang out the American National Anthem during a three minutes' silence.

WOOL EXCHANGE BUILDING

As a symbol of Bradford's great wealth in the mid-19th century, perhaps one of its finest buildings is the Wool Exchange, which stands in the heart of the city. This fine building was completed in 1857 and designed by the firm of architects, Lockwood and Mawson, who were to design many of Bradford's exquisite buildings, including the City Hall and the famous Salt's Mill. Again, as prevalent at that time, the contract was won through open competition. The foundation stone was laid in 1864 by Lord Palmerston, the Prime Minister of the time. Around the circumference of the building are carved busts of famous men in history such as Raleigh, Drake and Columbus to name but a few. Flanking the canopied entrance are the statues of Bishop Blaise (the patron saint of wool combers) and King Edward III (who had done so much to encourage the wool trade).

Today this building is no longer a wool exchange, but it now houses a variety of shops, including a book shop and newsagents. There is also a coffee-house on the mezzanine floor that offers excellent views of the fine interior architecture and overlooks a statue of Richard Cobden. Although not born in Yorkshire, Cobden was for many years MP for the West Riding of Yorkshire and a member of the Anti-Corn Law League. He maintained that this law was economically disastrous, morally wrong and prevented free trade.

The Wool Exchange in Bradford – statue of Edward III, who had actively encouraged the growth of the wool trade.

Little Germany, Bradford.

LITTLE GERMANY

So named because of the number of German merchants who traded there, Little Germany was and still is one of Bradford's busiest commercial areas, with the buildings dating back to the mid-19th century. Many of the

Little Germany.

buildings were imposing warehouses that the merchants had built to store and from which to sell their goods. Julius Delius (father of the composer), a prosperous businessman who had originally come from Germany, had his warehouse located here. Little Germany holds one of the finest collections of Victorian warehouses in Britain and was designated an area of conservation in 1973. There is currently much renovation taking place in the area.

UNDERCLIFFE CEMETERY

With the coming of the Industrial Age came a rapid growth in the population of Bradford. More people inevitably meant more deaths, and Bradford at the time was notorious for being a filthy town. Diseases such as scarlet fever, cholera and typhoid were deadly killers and were rife amongst the expanding population. The average life expectancy for the working classes was just 17 years and about double that for the gentry. Prior to the boom brought on by mechanisation, the parish church grounds were capable of accommodating the dead, but it soon became too full, and something urgently needed to be done. It was decided that a cemetery was needed that was both easy to access and on the outskirts of the town. A group of influential businessmen formed the Bradford Cemetery Group in 1849, and it originally had 13 directors, including such men as Sir Titus Salt. Although there was a pressing need for such an enterprise, it was from the outset also a business that was intended as very much a money-making venture.

The first concern for the Bradford Cemetery Group was to find land suitable for a cemetery, and soon such an area of land became available. A local wealthy Quaker family wanted to sell off their estate at Undercliffe, and on 16 July 1851 an auction took place to sell off almost 100 acres of farmland and buildings. The auction took place at the Sun Inn on Ivegate, and the land was divided into plots. The Bradford Cemetery Group

Undercliffe Cemetery.

purchased two plots covering 26 acres at a cost of £3,400. Two men were employed to turn this land into a cemetery – William Gay as the designer and John Dale was to be the architect. The total cost of the project was to be £12,000 and was to include a registrar's house and office, a gardener's and sexton's lodge, and two chapels – one for Anglicans and the other for Dissenters. Some existing buildings were to remain for the use of stone masons. The first person to be interred in Undercliffe Cemetery was Ann Scarf, spinster of Little Horton, who died at the age of 22.

In life the Victorians had a taste for the ornate and many of their buildings displayed a grandeur befitting a rich nation, with intricate carvings and colonnades that would not have been out of place on palaces. The Victorians would continue this fashion into death, and walking around Undercliffe Cemetery the visitor is immediately struck by the obvious show of wealth and pomp, with many burial plots worthy of kings. Today, with the cemetery well cared for and the monuments restored, it is hard to believe that only recently things could have been so different. With the insolvency of the Bradford Cemetery

Company in 1976 things rapidly went into decline, and it was not long before the cemetery was to fall prey to vandals and thieves. Over the years the situation grew worse, and Bradford nearly lost this remarkable site forever, until in the early 1980s it was decided that enough was enough and something had to be done. After three years of continuous campaigning the cemetery was compulsory purchased from its then owner (a property developer) and was given Conservation Order status. This was far from the end of the story, however, and two years after work had commenced to save the cemetery it was abandoned yet again. A new organisation took over, the Undercliffe Cemetery Charity, a registered charity. In 1998 the cemetery gained English Heritage recognition and became a listed area.

Originally the Bradford Cemetery Group had been formed out of need to bury the dead of a rapidly expanding population and provide an adequate site as a cemetery. The 26 acres at Undercliffe had more than amply filled that and was to provide enough space for 23,000 graves and the last resting place of some 123,880 people.

WILLIAM EDWARD FORSTER

Although not a native of Bradford, William Edward Forster was to make it his home. Born on 11 July 1818 to Quaker parents at Bradpole in Dorset, he was educated at a Friends' school at Tottenham. After leaving school, he went into the woollen trade in Bradford. He married in 1850, but his wife, not being a Quaker, caused him to be excommunicated. The Friends who delivered the sentence to him 'shook hands and stayed for luncheon', for as private friends they heartily congratulated him on his forthcoming marriage. Although it is said that from that moment on William considered himself a member of the Church of England, he still attended meetings of the society and always retained a deep interest in their welfare. Years later when a delegation of Quakers had been waiting upon him in his ministerial capacity, he told them, 'Your people turned me out of the society for doing the best thing I ever did in my life.' The couple had no children themselves, but when his wife's brother died leaving four orphans they adopted them as their own. Forster moved to Bradford in 1841 and became a partner with William Fison in a woollen manufacturing business. This partnership was to last until Forster's death, and the business would be carried on by their respective sons Frederick W. Fison and E.P. Arnold-Forster.

It was while accompanying his father to distribute relief funds in 1846 to the victims of the Great Famine in Ireland that Forster developed his philanthropic beliefs. This led him to taking an active interest in public affairs by delivering speeches and lectures. In 1859 he stood unsuccessfully as the Liberal candidate for Leeds. He was highly regarded in West Yorkshire, however, and two years later he was elected unopposed for Bradford. Over the next few years he enjoyed an active role in Parliament, but it is perhaps for his work on education reform that he will be best remembered. On 17 February 1870 the Elementary Education Bill was passed, also commonly known as Forster's Education Act. The bill set out the framework for schooling of all children in England and Wales between the ages of five and 13, but it was not popular with everybody, and many remained hostile to mass education, believing that it would make the working class think and consequently become dissatisfied with their lives. This, they felt, may lead to revolution. Others thought, however, that a general education could lead to the indoctrination of the working class.

William Edward Forster's political career was not without its controversy. In 1881 he introduced a bill to deal with the Land League in Ireland. The bill enabled the Irish Government to arrest without trial anyone 'reasonably suspected' of crime and conspiracy. During the course of his speech, while introducing the bill, he declared that it was 'the most painful duty'. Forster was nicknamed 'Buckshot' by the national press, as they believed he had ordered the police to fire on a crowd. Forster's life was in danger, though several attempts to murder him came to nothing. Lord Fredrick Cavendish, his successor, was not so lucky, however, and was murdered in Dublin. W.E. Forster died on 6 April 1886, on the eve of the First Home Rule Bill. He had been described by Gladstone as a 'man upon whom there could be no doubt that Nature had laid her hand for the purpose of forming a thoroughly genuine and independent character.' A man that was either loved or loathed by those who knew him, there would be no middle ground, and some of his severest critics were also his closest friends.

Built in the late 19th century, Forster Square pays tribute to this great man. Until the late 1950s the square was spacious with public gardens and his statue in the centre. Then much of the centre of Bradford underwent re-development and the square saw a number of changes. The re-development was the brainchild of Stanley Gordon Wardley, City Engineer for Bradford during the 1950s and 1960s. His idea was a new city 'with a provision for a continuous flow of self-regulating traffic'. Very much a man of his age, he rejected the traditional sandstone in favour of more modern materials for his buildings. Many of the beautiful and much-loved buildings were torn down to make way for his vision of the 'city of the future'. Many protested in vain about this destruction.

On 18 March 2004 Forster Square was completely cleared to make room for new development. The statue of Forster, which stands 9ft tall and was cast from over two tonnes of bronze, has been removed for safe keeping, and it is planned that it will eventually be replaced when the work is complete. After the clearance, the site remained empty for three years. Work eventually commenced at the beginning of 2008. One of the biggest benefits of this demolition is the opportunity it has offered to archaeologists to learn more about this city. Traces of 16th-century buildings have been unearthed and smaller finds have been found, such has coins, pottery, clay-pipes, a bone spoon and a bone tooth brush. This is the first time that archaeologists have been able to undergo some real field excavations in the centre of Bradford, and as such its importance should not be underestimated.

LISTER'S MILL

Standing proudly on the Bradford skyline is Lister's Mill. The size of this great mill simply dwarfs all other buildings for miles around. It is not hard to believe that on its completion in 1873 it was the largest textile mill in the North of England. Still breath-taking today, it must have been totally awe-inspiring in its day. Built in the Italianate style, which was so popular at the time of construction, it has a single 255ft chimney that can be seen from almost anywhere in Bradford.

Lister's Mill chimney.

At the turn of the 19th century Bradford was a rural market town and the woollen trade was still only a cottage industry. Within as little as 40 years, however, there were 38 worsted mills in Bradford, and by 1850 it had become the wool capital of the world. Many industrialists were to make their fortunes through the woollen industry and with their wealth built the cities and towns of West Yorkshire into living monuments to their achievements. One such industrialist was Samuel Cunliffe Lister, who was born on 1 January 1815 at Calverley Hall near Bradford. His father, Ellis Cunliffe Lister (1774–1853), was elected the first Member of Parliament for Bradford.

In 1838 Samuel started a business with his elder brother John to produce worsted goods in a mill that their father had built for them at Manningham. It was to prove very successful and was to bring Lister much fame and fortune. During the mid-1850s he began to experiment with the fibres contained in silk waste. After a number of years, he managed

Lister's Mill.

successfully to produce a machine for silk-combing, but not before becoming almost bankrupt in the process. He also perfected a loom to weave velvet, which was to make him rich. In 1871 the original Manningham Mills (also known as Lister's Mill) was destroyed by fire, and Samuel Lister replaced it with a new mill, which was to become the largest silk mill in the world. At its height 11,000 men, women and children were employed at the mill, producing high-quality fabrics such as velvet and silk. During World War Two the mill was to produce over 4,000 miles worth of parachute silk. Silk is no longer produced at the mill as Lister's fell into decline in the 1980s, and today this magnificent mill has been converted into luxury apartments.

POOR LAW OFFICES AND BRADFORD REGISTER OFFICE

In 1834 the Poor Law Amendment Act was passed, which allowed parishes to form unions to be jointly responsible for the administration and funding of the Poor Law in their area. Boards of Guardians were formed to ensure that the functions of the Poor Law Unions were exercised correctly.

The origins of a Poor Law system went back as far as Tudor times, when attempts were made to tackle the situation of the poor during the reign of Henry VII. A statute had been passed by Parliament empowering officials to arrest all vagabonds and the unemployed; as no distinction was made between the two, both were simply termed 'sturdy beggars'. Once seized, they would then be taken to the stocks, where they would remain for a period of three days, surviving on bread and water. After that period, they would be removed from the stocks and kicked out of the town, no doubt to move on to the next town or village to endure the same treatment. Although this system was not really a remedy for the problem of poverty, it was a way of papering over the cracks by keeping the vagabonds on the move.

Henry VIII was to issue a proclamation in 1530, in which he stated that idleness was the 'mother and root of all evil'. He replaced the stocks with whipping as a punishment for vagabonds. He did, however, make the distinction between 'sturdy beggars' and those considered 'impotent poor'; the sick, the old and the disabled. Those unable to work due to infirmity were given licence to beg. There was no provision for a healthy man who simply could not find work; he was left with a stark choice between starving or breaking the law. Things would get even tougher for him during the reign of Edward VI, when a bill was passed that would result in vagrants facing a two-year prison sentence and also to be branded with a 'V'. For their second offence they could face the death penalty. The law was so severe that many Justices of the Peace were reluctant to apply it. We have no evidence that the act was ever enforced, and it was eventually repealed in 1550.

Elizabeth I was to reintroduce the death sentence as a punishment for persistent beggars. In an act passed in 1572 a distinction between

Bradford Register Office.

'professional' beggars and those who were simply unemployed was made for the first time. This eventually led to the provision for the deserving poor with the introduction of the Elizabethan Poor Law.

For many reasons both the Elizabethan Poor Law and the Poor Law Amendment Act of 1834 were opposed. This opposition came from a wide range of social classes; from paupers and workers, to the academics and the landed gentry. One of the conditions of the Poor Law Amendment was that anyone wishing poor relief must enter the workhouse. The workhouse (also known as a 'spike') inspired many fears and rumours. Usually built at some distance from industrial centres, it was rumoured that they were extermination centres to reduce the numbers of paupers and keep taxes low. It was also rumoured that they were places of cheap labour, used to keep the national wage bill down. A pamphlet entitled the *Book of Murder* was widely circulated. It was believed by some to be the work of the Poor Law commission as it advocated infanticide; however, it was a piece of Anti-Poor Law propaganda that had been penned by Joshua Hobson. Born in Huddersfield in 1810, Joshua Hobson first trained as a joiner, before moving near Oldham to become a handloom weaver. He was to spend some time in prison for his pamphlet printing activities, and between 1838 and 1844 he was to publish the *Northern Star*, a newspaper dedicated to the Chartist Movement.

One of the functions that the Poor Law Unions were later to take on was that of civil registration, namely, the registration of births, deaths and marriages. During the reign of Henry VIII there was an attempt to create registers, when Thomas Cromwell instructed the clergy of every parish throughout England and Wales to keep registers of baptisms, burials and marriages. In 1597 Elizabeth I repeated this Injunction with the added requirement that all registers 'be sent to a diocesan registrar' for protection. There were also penalties for neglect of this duty. This act was unsuccessful, however, as insufficient details were recorded in the registers, and there were also problems with security and storage. For the next few hundred years these records were kept in parish registers. In 1832 a 'Select Committee' decided that the whole system should be administered from a General National Office, which led to the 1836 Registration Act and the Marriage Act. It was on 1 July 1837 that both Acts were enforced and the Register Office came into being.

THE RAGGED SCHOOL

As the 19th century developed, education was seen as increasingly important. At the beginning of the century very few children went to school. Certainly schools for the lower classes were few and far between. Those lucky enough to attend would be taught reading and spelling, possibly writing as well, and the children of the middle-class families might receive a slightly better education, which could include arithmetic. The ruling classes considered it to be dangerous to educate the lower classes and consequently placed many obstacles in their way, preventing them from receiving adequate schooling if any at all.

By heavily taxing the necessities of life, the ruling classes were able to reduce the purchasing power of the workers. Although wages were kept low by law, they could be effectively reduced even further by increasing taxes. As well as taxing the necessities, such as food, other commodities, for example paper, were also heavily taxed. This in turn meant that books were expensive, especially school textbooks. A newspaper had a stamp duty of four pence upon each copy. At that time the common writing implement was the quill, which required skill to turn it into a good pen. An extremely sharp knife was required to produce a good pen from a quill, but this would have cost a fair amount of money, and few would have been able to afford the expense. Consequently, writing was seen as a luxury that only the well-off could do.

It was not just the rich, however, who were reluctant to provide education for the children of the working classes – in many cases it was the parents themselves. Education was seen by many as a frivolous waste of time, which only the rich could afford. It was thought that it would not better their lives and would be unnecessary for their future jobs. In reality many families needed the money that an extra pair of hands could bring in, albeit the hands of a child. But it was through the tireless work of people such as Richard Oastler that things began to gradually change, so whereas at the beginning of the 19th century it was unusual for a child to go to school, by the end of the century it was unusual for a child not to do so.

Introduced in the 1840s, the Ragged Schools were places where the children from the poorest districts could go to get an education. Charles Dickens described them as places where children could go who were 'too ragged, wretched, filthy, and forlorn, to enter any other place.' The children would be taught by local working people who held their classes in any buildings that were affordable, such as stables, lofts and railway arches. They were taught the three R's – reading, writing and arithmetic, plus bible study. There would eventually be 200 of these schools throughout the country, teaching approximately 300,000 children. Bradford was to open its own Ragged School at Cropper Lane in 1854.

BRADFORD SWEET POISONING

During the 19th century the adulteration of foodstuffs for financial gain was a common practice. This was to lead to dire consequences in 1858, when an estimated 20 people were to die through arsenic poisoning. William Hardaker, known locally as 'Humbug Billy', ran a confectionery stall in the Green Market. He purchased his stock locally from Joseph Neal, who made the sweets. The lethal sweets were peppermint humbugs, made from peppermint oil, gum and sugar; however, as sugar was an expensive ingredient it was not used, and it was normal for the confectioner to use a less costly alternative. The substitute ingredient was known as a 'daft', and its identity would vary depending on availability; plaster of Paris, powdered limestone and sulphate of lime being common alternatives.

On this occasion Joseph Neal had sent James Archer, who was lodging with him at the time, to collect the 'daft' from the pharmacist. The pharmacist in question was Charles Hodgson, whose premises were located at Baildon Bridge, Shipley. Unfortunately, at the time Hodgson was ill and unable to see Archer in person so his assistant William Goddard dealt with his request. Unable to locate the 'daft' he went to Hodgson and was told it was in the corner of the cellar in a cask. However rather than selling 'daft' he accidently sold 12lbs of arsenic trioxide, a highly toxic compound of arsenic. Oblivious to the error, the arsenic was added to the sweet mix by James Appleton, an experienced sweet-maker. He did observe that the finish of the sweets looked a little different but thought little of it, even though he began to feel unwell as he was making them. In total 40lbs of the sweets were sold to Hardaker who, complaining about their appearance, was able to get a discount. Hardaker tasting one of the sweets, promptly became ill, but this did not deter him from selling them and he sold 5lbs of them that very evening. Twenty people died as a result of eating the contaminated sweets, and around another 200 became extremely ill.

Initially, it was thought that the deaths had been caused by cholera, which was a major problem in Bradford at the time. However, as the number of casualties mounted, the cause of this outbreak of illness soon was traced back to

Hardaker's stall. It was not long before the trail had led to Neal, Hodgson and Goddard. All three were committed for trial on a charge of manslaughter, but the prosecution withdrew charges against Goddard and Neal, and Hodgson was acquitted. It had been estimated that each sweet contained about nine grains of arsenic – 4.5 grains being a lethal dose. The public outcry over this tragedy was eventually to lead to passing of the Pharmacy Act of 1868, and further legislation was brought in to tighten up controls on the adulteration of foodstuffs.

SALTAIRE AND SIR TITUS SALT

Opinions differ as to the motives of Sir Titus Salt; some say that he was a philanthropist who was concerned over the welfare of his workers, while others believe that he was a canny businessman who built Saltaire so as to have his workforce on tap. Regardless of opinions, however, there is no denying that he left an enduring legacy, and the impressive 'model' village that he built is now designated a World Heritage Site by UNESCO. In the 1980s Salt's Mill was converted into a gallery by the late Jonathan Silver, which houses a major collection of David Hockney's work, shops, restaurants and a theatre. Jonathan was a schoolboy in the 1960s when he first met the artist. Working on the school magazine, he persuaded David to design the cover. They had both kept in touch over the years, and when Jonathan bought the mill in 1987 he thought it would be an ideal showcase for David's work.

Sir Titus Salt was born in Morley near Leeds on 20 September 1803, and according to an entry written in the family Bible this happy event took place at four o'clock in the morning. His father, Daniel Salt, was a relatively successful businessman as a 'drysalter', a business he had inherited from his father-in-law. He also owned an iron foundry based in Hunslet, Leeds, which he had inherited from his father. Daniel was a plain and blunt Yorkshireman, both in manner and speech, but he was also a man of great energy and drive. Titus Salt went to Heath Grammar School in Halifax. The school had

Far right: Salt's Mill.

Statue of Sir Titus Salt at Robert's Park, Saltaire.

Salt's Mill was ideally placed, being built by the canal.

been founded by Dr John Favour in 1585, and its full title was The Free Grammar School of Queen Elizabeth (in 1985 the school merged to form Crossley Heath School). After leaving school, he spent a brief spell working for a Wakefield woolstapler until 1824 when he joined the family firm as a wool buyer. He took over the running of the business when his father retired in 1833.

Over the next 20 years he built up the business until he was the largest employer in Bradford. At the time Bradford had gained the grim reputation of being the most polluted town in England, and life expectancy was just over 18 years. Cholera and typhoid was common as sewage was poured into the River Beck, which was also the source of drinking water. As a major employer Salt was concerned with the health problems caused by the pollution and created the Rodda Smoke Burner, which he discovered produced far fewer pollutants than conventional methods. Becoming Mayor of Bradford in 1848, he tried in vain to pass a by-law that would enforce the use of the new burner, but sadly he was unsuccessful. Undeterred, he decided to leave Bradford and build his 'model' village on the banks of the River Aire near Shipley and to call

it Saltaire. Construction started in 1850, and it took 20 years to complete. At the centre of his showpiece village stood the mill. This ground-breaking mill had many innovations to make the conditions for his workforce markedly more comfortable and healthy. The shafts that drove the machinery were placed underground to reduce noise, large ducts removed the dust and dirt from the factory floor and, of course, the Rodda Smoke Burners were fitted to the chimney. Initially the workforce had to travel each day from Bradford, but over time he had 850 homes constructed near to the mill. Not only did he cater for the physical health of his workers by providing a healthier environment, but he also catered for their mental and spiritual health with the provision of a library and church; however, as he was a strict abstainer from alcohol there was an absence of public houses in Saltaire (though it is reputed that he did enjoy a glass of wine with his dinner).

In some ways Sir Titus Salt was a contradiction, an active reformer involved in politics and concerned about the workers' welfare. He supported the reduction of the working hours and was a severe critic of the 1834 Poor Law, but he refused permission for his workers to join a trade union and was also opposed to any legislation that prevented children under nine working in his factories. He was a man of few words, and he would often sit silently when in the company of strangers. His use of the wool, or perhaps more correctly hair, from the alpaca (an animal native to Peru) brought him widespread fame and even led to an amusing story written by Charles Dickens in a publication called *Household Words,* where the main character of the tale was based on Sir Titus Salt and his discovery of the unwanted bales of alpaca in a Liverpool warehouse. During his life he had been an extremely rich man, but his family were horrified to discover that on his death on 29 December 1879 his fortune had gone – it had been spent on good causes.

Church at Saltaire.

In 1877 the Revd R. Balgarnie wrote in his biography of the great man: 'The indirect results of Mr Titus Salt's achievements are so interwoven with the growth of Bradford, in population, in building, in trade and commerce, in moral and intellectual improvements, that it is impossible to separate the one from the other.' What more can be said?

FREDERICK DELIUS

Frederick Delius was born in Bradford on 29 January 1862. He was the fourth child of Julius and Elise Delius and had been christened Fritz Theodore Albert Delius. In later life he was to use the name Frederick instead of Fritz, and it is said that he dropped the name of Theodore after finding himself laughing during his confirmation. Theodore means 'beloved of God'. His father was a wool broker who had originally come from Bielefeld in Germany. Although a generous man with a kind heart, he was a Prussian in the fullest sense and demanded complete obedience from his family. He helped to found the Bradford Children's Hospital. Despite an obsession with money, he was prepared to spend vast sums on his children.

Frederick's scholarly life was not particularly distinguished, and with his brother Max he was to spend more time as a truant than at his studies. The only subject that could keep his attention was music. His father paid little attention to Frederick's growing love of music, believing the boy should indulge himself while he could, for he would have little time for this frivolity when he joined the family firm. Frederick had made no secret of his loathing for the business, but he intended to give it a fair trial. He told his sisters, however, that if he failed he would give his life to music and make the Delius name famous. After joining the firm, the young Frederick was initially sent to Stroud, where followed a period of apparent success. Shortly afterwards he was sent to Europe, where

he took every opportunity to further his musical experience, at the expense of his commercial activities, and it was not long before Julius was receiving discouraging reports. Frederick was summoned home.

He was able to persuade his ever-hopeful father to send him to Scandinavia as a representative of the firm. This too proved to be a failure, but it did result in him falling permanently under the spell of the North. Again he was recalled by his father, who took him to task. He was then sent to St Etienne, which was the centre of the French wool trade. As a way of restricting his irresponsible lifestyle, his father kept him short of money. Frederick was able to get around this tactic by gambling all he had on the tables at Monte Carlo. This proved successful enough for him to fund his musical ambitions. His father learnt of his extravagances, and yet again he was to receive a telegram recalling him. This time, however, probably much to his surprise and relief, he was sent to Scandinavia. Once again this was to end in failure, and no doubt his father was by this time at the end of his tether. Julius was a determined businessman and it appears that he did not know the meaning of defeat. So, undeterred, he sent his wayward son to his Uncle Ernst, where he was put in charge of his uncle's business for one day. The experience was enough to convince Frederick once and for all that he was not suited to this business.

In 1884 at the age of 22 he was invited to join Charles Douglas, the son of a Bradford dyer, on an adventure to Florida to grow oranges. He jumped at the chance, and with much persuasion he managed to eventually convince his furious father to the merits of the idea. In March of that year the pair sailed for Florida and the Solana Grove plantation. It was while on the plantation that Douglas became ill with malaria, and Frederick went to seek help of a doctor. The nearest doctor was 20 miles away at Jacksonville. Frederick arrived to find that the doctor was not at home, and to while away the time he found a music shop with a piano. This would prove a turning point in his life, for as he played the piano an organist from New York passed the shop. After hearing Frederick play, he entered the shop and introduced himself as Thomas F. Ward. Delius immediately forgot his sick friend and stayed in Jacksonville for several days.

Furious at his friend's neglect, Douglas left the plantation, and although Frederick had lost a partner he had gained a teacher. Thomas was to give Delius lessons in orchestration, counterpoint and fugue, which he was to work at with a dedication hitherto unknown for him. In July 1884 Julius bought the plantation with the idea of keeping Frederick dependent on him. It was at this time that Frederick conceived the idea of going to Leipzig to further his musical education. Unfortunately, now that his father owned the plantation he felt that he was somewhat tied by duty to remain. It was the arrival of his brother Ernst from New Zealand that was to dramatically change things and give him the opportunity of following his dreams. His brother had arrived penniless and took little persuading to relinquish his sheep farming in favour of oranges.

Eventually settling in Paris, Delius met Ravel, Gauguin and Strindberg. It was at this time that he began his custom of holidaying in Norway. He wrote his first major work between 1890 and 1892, the opera *Irmelin*. In 1903 Delius married Jelka Rosen, a painter whose family had come from Schleswig-Holstein. They had common interests in Grieg's music and Nietzsche. His father died a couple of years earlier at the age of 80, without ever acknowledging his son's musical achievements. Frederick received no mention in his father's will, though he was to receive £550 from the residual estate. It was in 1904 that recognition was at last achieved with the production of *Koanga*, an opera with a voodoo theme. This was followed in 1906 by *Sea Drift*, and the following year he at last found recognition in England with the performance of

his *Piano Concerto*. His work *North Country Sketches* was to show that he had never really severed all the links that still held him close to his Yorkshire roots. It was, in fact, his ambition to write an opera based on *Wuthering Heights*, which sadly never materialised.

In 1922 the first signs of his illness began to manifest themselves when he lost the use of both hands, and by 1927 he was completely blind and paralysed. It was in 1928 that the working relationship between him and Eric Fenby began. At first it seemed doomed to failure, for Delius thought that the young musician from Scarborough was useless, and it was largely due to the patient mediation of Jelka that the partnership survived. Fenby was completely in awe of Delius and his music. When, however, he ventured to criticise a piece which he felt inferior, Delius almost fell out of his chair. Calming down, he told Fenby to take the piece, select the best material and make it his own. This he did and after a week he performed it for Delius. This was the turning point in their relationship and with great emotion Delius said, 'Fenby, you are an artist! I can work with you. You have set my mind in action after all this time.'

Although Frederick's parents were both German and he lived most of his adult life abroad, his music pays homage to the land of his birth. His work is said to possess the freshness of the Yorkshire moors. Delius died on 10 June 1934. After a temporary burial, the coffin was exhumed and brought back to England, where he was reburied at midnight in a country churchyard at Limpsfield, Surrey. Delius had been a lifelong follower of Nietzsche and an atheist, never a man for prayers, and in accordance with his wishes there was no word of committal.

NEWLANDS MILL DISASTER

It was 8am on Thursday 28 December 1882, and the workers at Newlands Mill were having their morning breakfast break when disaster struck.

A massive 255ft-high chimney collapsed, killing 54 people. The chimney weighed 4,000 tonnes and had been in a precarious state for a number of years. The mill had been built on a site where there had once been extensive coal and iron mining. A warren of tunnels that ran under the buildings had meant that the chimney was extremely unstable. The problem had been aggravated as the chimney had been built directly over the old pit shaft, which had been filled with wood and debris.

By 1882 cracks were beginning to form in the chimney and an ominous bulge had developed. Occasionally bits of masonry had dropped off. Over the Christmas period some repairs to the structure had been undertaken, but it was too little too late. The death toll could have been much higher if it was not for the fact that many of the workers had gone home for their breakfast. Even so, many families were lost, and of those who survived a number received serious injuries. Today a memorial to the victims of this disaster can be found at the corner of St Stephen's Road and Gaythorne Road in West Bowling Bradford. This tribute is,

however, fairly new as for 120 years the tragedy was largely forgotten.

ANTHRAX AND FRIEDERICH WILHELM EURICH

First noticed in 1847, cutaneous anthrax or 'Wool-sorters' disease' became a major problem in the woollen mills of Bradford. On average there was one new case a week, and a third of these proved fatal. The cause of this scourge was the introduction of alpaca and mohair (angora goat hair) that was being imported from Central Asia. Early attempts to eradicate the infection were not effective, and it was not until the Bradford Anthrax Investigation Board, which had been set up in 1905, had instigated various medical and legal measures that the disease began to be controlled. In 1918 the Anthrax Prevention Act was passed, and the Wool Disinfecting Station was established at Liverpool. It was through the major contribution of Dr Friederich Wilhelm Eurich that these changes were possible.

Born in Chemnitz, Saxony, in 1867, he came to England at the age of seven. His father had

Statue of J.B. Priestley.

worked in the textile trade and had moved to the branch of a German yarn firm in Bradford. Friederich was educated at Bradford Grammar School. He trained as a doctor at Edinburgh and initially practised neurology at the Lancashire County Asylum. It was from there that he submitted his MD in 1897 and was to receive a gold medal, being one of only four to be awarded that year. In 1896 he set up a general practice in Bradford and was appointed honorary physician for the Bradford hospitals. As well as these posts he was to take up the position of class assistant to Professor H.J. Campbell, the Professor of Forensic Medicine at Leeds Medical School, where he provided supervision to the medical students of practical toxicology.

In 1900 a Pathological and Bacteriological Laboratory was established in Bradford and Eurich was appointed bacteriologist. Five years later the Bradford Anthrax Investigation Board was established in Morley Street and he became bacteriologist to the board. When Professor Campbell resigned in 1908, Eurich successfully applied for the position. The work entailed 40 lectures, all to be given during the autumn term and acting as internal examiner twice a year. For this position he was to receive an honorarium of £38 per year, which never increased over the years he held the post. He was to retire in 1932 after many successful years as a popular teacher, throughout which he achieved outstanding results. The *Yorkshire Observer* stated, on his death in 1945, that he 'did so much to conquer the disease of anthrax and whose contributions in the cause of medicine were so outstanding.'

J.B. PRIESTLEY

Born on 13 September 1894 in Bradford, John Boynton Priestley was a prolific writer and broadcaster. Although perhaps best known as a playwright and novelist, J.B. Priestley was also very active in politics, and he became the chairman of the 1941 Committee, which included such people as Michael Foot and

Kingsley Martin. The group advocated the public control of railways, mines and docks and also a national wages policy. On 26 July 1941 J.B. Priestley, with a few other members of the committee, formed the Common Wealth Party, but after only winning one seat in the 1945 General Election the party dissolved and most of its members joined the Labour Party. He continued to write about politics and gained quite a following of readers who supported his views. J.B. Priestley was also one of the founding members of the Campaign for Nuclear Disarmament. He died on 14 August 1984, and today his statue can be seen outside the National Museum of Photography, Film & Television in Bradford.

ALHAMBRA

Perhaps one of the most distinctive buildings in Bradford is the Alhambra Theatre, built for the impresario Francis Laidler in 1914. It was constructed on waste land by Chadwick and Watson, a firm of architects based in Leeds who were renowned for their classical cinema designs. When the Alhambra first opened, the era of the Music Hall was giving way to the more family

the ground floor and all the seats were upholstered to the same standards, whether they were in the pit, stalls or dress circle. Although the theatre has a Moorish name (Alhambra is derived from Kal'-at al hambra, meaning 'The Red Castle'), its décor is in the style of Louis XVI.

After the death of Francis Laidler in 1955, his widow, Gwladys Stanley, took over control of his theatres. The Alhambra Company went into liquidation in the mid-1960s, at which point Bradford City Council bought the theatre. In the early 1980s the Alhambra faced an uncertain future; there were even plans to demolish it and place a car-park there instead. But in 1986 the building was saved, and much restoration took place, including extending the building, which now incorporates a stage that is twice as large as the original.

One of the stone lions, which were carved by Alfred Broadbent, a local sculptor from Shipley, standing guard over Queen Victoria's monument. In the background stands the distinctively shaped Alhambra theatre.

orientated 'variety', which was a less vulgar form of entertainment. To capitalise on these changes Francis Laidler wanted a building that would become Bradford's premier palace of pantomime. The theatre was capable of seating 1,800 people and had a stage that was 35ft wide. This truly opulent building had thick carpets on

JUDY WOODS

Judy Woods is the collective name of a number of woodlands: Doctor Wood, Gannerthorpe, Jagger Park Wood, Low Wood, Neddy Wood, North Brow Wood, Old Hanna Wood, Royds Hall Great Wood and the Sun & Shelf Woods.

Judy Woods.

Ancient packhorse route in Jagger woods – this would have been the motorway of its day.

The woodland stands on coal-bearing land and therefore was a significant area during the Industrial Revolution. Evidence of the extraction of coal can be seen by the numerous bell pits which can be found in the woods. It is thought that at one time the woodland would have been much larger and even possibly have been part of the extensive Bryanscholes Forest which is said to have reached as far as Sherwood Forest.

ROYDS HALL MANOR

In close proximity to Judy Woods lies Royds Hall Manor. This impressive stone building, one of the best examples of a manor house in Bradford, was constructed in 1640 over the half-timbered building that previously stood there. A cartouche can be seen, dating from 1640, with the initials W.R. standing for William Rooke, who was responsible for the central portion of the building that comprises two halls.

The estate belonged to the Rookes family who, although originally only tenants of the land, were later granted ownership of it for service to the Crown. The hall remained in the Rookes family until the late 18th century when Edward Rookes (who had changed his name to Rookes Leedes when he married a wealthy heiress Mary Leedes) died in 1785.

The area was rich in mineral deposits, and Edward gained a considerable income from coal mining. Four years after his death the Low Moor Company bought the estate. The Revd Joseph Dawson, a trained mineralogist, was the master technologist behind the company and lived at Royds Hall until his death in 1813.

THE LOW MOOR EXPLOSION

In August 1914 World War One began, and what was to follow was four years of carnage. It soon became apparent that this was to be a war like no other; this was to be a war that was waged from trenches, over barren fields of mud and barbed wire. For the first time machines would be brought into the field of conflict – tanks and

Together they make up the third–largest woodland area in Bradford. It was a seller of 'Sweet Meats' in the mid-19th century who gave her name to the woods – Judy North or 'Gurt Judy' lived in a cottage near Horse Close Bridge. Judy was very much a character, and on one occasion she caught the local vicar taking a plant from her garden. She confronted him and demanded payment for the plant, only to be told that she would receive her money once it was proved to be thriving in his garden. She was, however, to have the last laugh when she took a baby boy to be baptised and withheld the vicar's fee, stating that she would only pay it when it became clear that the child would grow into a strong lad, reputedly saying to the vicar, 'before I pay I must wait and see whether t'bairn thrives or not, as ye did wi' my plant.' He grew to be over 6ft tall and was of massive build. There is a story told about him as a young man that tells of the time he was offered a young rabbit if he could put the whole thing in his mouth, complete with skin. This he apparently succeeded in doing.

This 16in rolling mill flywheel from the former Low Moor Steel Works weighs a little over 30 tonnes and was donated to Bradford Council in 1982. It now stands as a monument at Low Moor.

airplanes. Britain was woefully ill-prepared to fight this war of attrition and desperately needed a solution. This was to be the high-explosive shell. The French had originally used high-explosive shells in 1886. They had used picric acid instead of gunpowder, which when detonated proved to be a powerful explosive. The British Army were soon to adopt the use of picric, which they were to call lyddite.

Another use of picric acid was as a dyestuff, especially in the manufacture of carpets. In 1898 the Low Moor Chemical Company began to manufacture picric acid. It was not long, though, before the company was selling the acid for the bursting charge for shells, and on 1 September 1898 they gained their first licence to produce explosives. Their production capacity grew until they were one of the largest manufacturers of lyddite in the country. At the beginning of World War One they were renamed the Low Moor Munitions Company, and the Ministry of Munitions gave them the designation 'Factory No182, Yorkshire'. Although the production of picric acid was a dangerous process, it appears that the company had been fairly accident free,

that is until Monday 21 August 1916. The war had just started its second year, and the Battle of the Somme, perhaps the most infamous of all battles, had commenced at the beginning of July. Demands for picric acid would have been high, and there is no doubt that there would have been efforts to increase production.

At the time of the explosion there were about 30,000lbs of picric acid waiting to be sampled and then shipped, and with even more still being processed. The explosion was caused by a fire that had broken out in a drum of the acid. A number of uncovered drums were being transported from one the sheds where the acid was dried to the magazines. According to one witness, as he was unloading the drums he heard a 'sizzling noise', and he turned around just in time to see one of the unloaded drums burst into flames. The force from it was enough to knock him off his feet. It was not long before the flames had spread into the magazine. The air was thick with dust from the crushing machines used on the acid crystals, and there is no doubt that this dust would have accelerated the spread of the flames. By mid-afternoon the magazine was ablaze, and moments later it exploded, blowing wood, bricks and iron pipes into the air. The debris covered a wide area, with a large piece of twisted metal landing in a field over a mile away.

The City's Engineer and Surveyor's Office estimated that around 2,000 private houses in the surrounding area had been affected, with about 50 being almost totally destroyed. The explosions were to continue for two days, with about 22 on the Monday. It took three days for the fires to be put out. A fire engine named *Hayhurst* was completely destroyed and six of her crew killed when caught in one of the explosions. The newly acquired fire engine had just arrived at the scene, and the crew were connecting hoses when it was caught in the blast. As well as the damage to the private houses, the munitions factory was severely damaged, the local dye works almost gutted, two gasometers destroyed, Low Moor Iron Works was badly damaged and rolling stock on the sidings was also damaged by fire. A total of 37 men lost their lives in the tragedy at Low Moor. It was thought at the time that it may have been an act of sabotage that caused this dreadful disaster. Among the workers were a number of

Belgian refugees, and a popular theory at the time was that German spies and saboteurs may have infiltrated them. After some careful investigations this explanation was rejected. Picric acid reacts with most metals to produce picrates, which are more volatile than the acid itself. One metal that it does not react with is tin. The drums used were tin-plated, and it is thought that over time the tin wore away to expose the iron beneath. This in turn could have led to the formation of picrates, which are sensitive to percussion and could have been ignited as the drums were moved. It is doubtful, however, that we will ever know what really happened on that sunny Monday in the summer of 1916.

HAWORTH & THE BRONTËS

No book on West Yorkshire would be complete without mention of Haworth and the Brontë family, whose name is for evermore synonymous with the picturesque village and the wild surrounding moors. This popular village, nestling on a steep slope above the Worth valley between Cullingworth Moor and Penistone Hill, attracts visitors from all over the

Opposite: Sun rising over Haworth's main street.

Brontë Falls.

world. Steeped in history, the village is a sensitive fusion between the traditional and the modern with many delightful attractions for the visitor. Walk up the steep cobbled main street and one is instantly whisked away to another era. Even without its connection to the Brontë family, Haworth would still be a fascinating village to visit in its own right.

It took a hardy type to survive in this windswept place of moorland and heather. Haworth was a crowded and unhygienic place in the mid-19th century. Without sewers and with a polluted water supply the mortality rate was extremely high. Strolling around its streets today, breathing the fresh clean air blowing in

off the moors, it is hard to believe that at one time it had one of the highest mortality rates in Britain. During a 10-year period between 1840 and 1850 there were over 1,300 burials, and the average life expectancy was 25 years.

The Brontë children, Charlotte, Branwell, Emily and Anne, were all born at Thornton, which is now a suburb of Bradford. In 1820, when Charlotte was nearly five, their father Patrick Brontë became appointed incumbent of Haworth. It was the wild land around Haworth which would have such a profound effect on the future literary careers of the three sisters who went on to produce such timeless classics as *Wuthering Heights* and *Jane Eyre*. Originally the family name was not Brontë but had been Brunty, and they had not come from Yorkshire – Patrick was born in Ireland in 1777, and his wife Maria had come from Cornwall. It was not long after the family had moved to Haworth when Mrs Brontë died from cancer. Her unmarried sister, Elizabeth Branwell, left her comfortable home in Penzance to take charge of running the Brontë household. In 1824 the sisters were sent to the Clergy Daughters' School at Cowan Bridge,

Breathtaking scenery – the path leading to Brontë Falls.

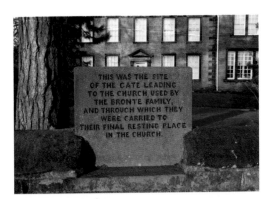

Far left: The Parsonage at Haworth.

near Kirkby Lonsdale; however, tragedy soon struck when the two eldest sisters Maria and Elizabeth were to die from illness within a short time of each other. After the death of the two girls, the remaining siblings were kept at home, where they created an imaginary world. Their father was keen that they would gain an education, and he encouraged them in this goal. They were insatiable readers, devouring any book that came their way.

In the 19th century there was only one socially acceptable occupation for a genteel young lady, and that was as a governess. This would mean that the sisters would need to acquire the skills which would enable them to follow this path. In 1831 Charlotte went to study at Miss Wooler's school at Roe Head, Mirfield. Eventually she became a teacher there and was to become teacher to her two younger sisters. For a brief time Emily was to teach at a school at Law Hill, Halifax. It was apparently not a happy time, and she is reported to have told her pupils that she 'preferred the school dog to them'. She was soon back home in Haworth. Disheartened with the life of governesses, the three sisters planned to set up a school in Haworth, but it had little success for they were unable to find sufficient pupils.

Branwell was the black sheep of the family – an alcoholic and opium user, who was unable to hold a job for long. Although better remembered for his hedonistic and self-destructive exploits, he too was a writer in his own right. Tragically, he eventually paid the ultimate price for his self abuse, and he died at the age of 31 from

Haworth was once reputed to have the highest mortality rate in the country.

tuberculosis. Emily Brontë was to die only three months later from the same cause – she was only 30. A month later Anne was to succumb to the same fate (aged 29), so this only left Charlotte. At the age of 38 Charlotte married Revd Arthur Bell Nichols, who was her father's curate. Patrick opposed the marriage because he did not think his curate a suitable match, as he regarded him as a poor Irish curate and his daughter was by now famous. Although the marriage was happy, it was short-lived as she died in the early stages of pregnancy, not 12 months after her wedding day. Given the mortality rate of the area, perhaps their early deaths are not so surprising but, as short as their lives were, they succeeded in producing literary masterpieces that will live on and on.

KEIGHLEY

As we have already seen with many of the other towns and villages of West Yorkshire, it is difficult to know when Keighley first became a settlement. Many artefacts have been found that date back to the Bronze and Iron Ages, which would suggest that man has had a long association with the area. We do have concrete evidence that there was a settlement prior to the compiling of the *Domesday Book*, when it was recorded as being called 'Chiceha'. Keighley is located 11 miles from Bradford and stands at the confluence of the River Aire and the River Worth. As with the majority of settlements throughout the whole of West Yorkshire, it was heavily into the textile industry – both woollen and cotton. Engineering was also important to the town's prosperity as there were a number of large factories producing machinery for the textile trade. As a consequence of the success of these industries, the population increased 10-fold from the beginning of the 19th century (when the population stood at 6,000) until 1850.

During the English Civil War, Keighley saw action at the Battle of Keighley in 1645. The battle took place between the Parliamentarians of Keighley and the Royalists of Skipton and resulted in a victory for Keighley, with the capturing of the Royalist commander and the killing of 15 of his troops. It is thought that the Roundheads kept their prisoner at a garrison just outside Keighley. There is an area still known to this day as Guardhouse, and it would not be too far-fetched to suggest that this might have been the location of the commander's incarceration. At the bottom of Oakworth Road, just outside the town, lies a field where it is believed the battle took place.

Keighley was first granted the right to hold a market when the lord of the manor received a charter from Edward I on 17 October 1305 – 'to hold a Market, Fair and Free Warren in Keighley'. In 1375 during the reign of Richard II the population of Keighley was only 115, and for many centuries it was smaller than many of its neighbours, including Haworth. In fact it was not until the growth experienced with the coming of the Industrial Age that it saw a rapid change in size. It appears that the earliest church to be built in Keighley was in the 13th

century, and there is certainly no mention of there being one in the *Domesday Book*.

Sadly the original mediaeval church no longer exists as it was demolished in 1805. During the demolition two stones were discovered – a tomb cover and a Celtic cross. The latter was possibly a preaching cross predating the construction of a church. The new church only lasted 40 years until it too was demolished to make way for the church that we can now see standing there. The present St Andrew's was built in the Victorian Gothic style and cost £7,000 to build. At the beginning of the 20th century a new entrance was constructed, and a clock was presented that chimed to the tune of *Lead me, Lord, in thy righteousness*. The Church Registers, dating back to 1562, are now kept safe with the West Yorkshire Archive Service.

In 1742 Methodism arrived at Keighley when John Wilkinson, a journeyman shoemaker, was converted. Each week a group of people would meet at his cottage to pray, sing psalms and hold discussions. After a few months he began to preach, and he soon had his first convert – a local businessman called Thomas Colbeck. It was not long before the initial group of people meeting in his cottage had swelled in numbers from 10 to 100. In 1746 John Wesley visited the town for the first time and met both Wilkinson and Colbeck. As the society grew, it became essential to find new premises to hold their weekly meetings. Thomas Colbeck purchased land on Temple Row, and the new Preaching House was built. The building was to be used for nearly 220 years, until in 1973, with dwindling membership and high cost of maintenance, the premises were sold to the local council. In 1982 a Methodist hall was opened in the grounds of the parish church, and since the loss of Temple Row both churches have shared buildings and worked together, eventually joining to become Keighley Shared Church.

In 1904 the first Carnegie Library in England

was to be built in Keighley. The £10,000 needed to construct the library had been donated by Andrew Carnegie, a rich Scottish-American businessman. A cornerstone of his belief was that the 'industrious and ambitious; not those who need everything done for them, but those who, being most anxious and able to help themselves, deserve and will be benefited by help from others.'

Eventually over 2,500 Carnegie Libraries were to be built throughout the world. Sadly the library at Keighley had suffered through much neglect but has recently undergone extensive refurbishment. Keighley possesses many fine examples of Victorian architecture, and being ideally located it is soon possible to discover stunning landscapes on its doorstep.

Over the centuries West Yorkshire has had its fair share of characters and eccentrics, and one worthy of a mention is James Leach, better known to all who knew him as 'Pie' Leach. An inhabitant of Keighley during the 19th century, 'Pie' Leach had at one time sold meat pies, hence his nickname. Several years before he passed away he had his tombstone prepared, onto which he had the account of his life and

achievements chiselled. Throughout his life he had undertaken a number of varied jobs. The eldest of five children, he started his job at the age of 10 as a handloom weaver. As a young man he earned a reputation for heavy drinking and gambling. Over time he altered his ways and became a respected citizen, and his proudest possession was a certificate stating his good character, which had been signed by the Rector of Keighley, the town's Police Superintendent, and three J.P.s.

A strong believer in the benefits of married life, he was to be wedded three times. His first marriage almost failed to take place, as he arrived just before it was time to lock the church door. He persuaded a friend to climb inside the church tower, and by stopping the clock the vicar was fooled into believing that the marriage was within the permitted hours. His last wedding took place when he was 76 years old, and his bride was 35. The ceremony took place at the local register office and drew large crowds of sightseers. It was only by police intervention that the crowds were stopped from unyoking the wedding carriage and dragging it to the home of the newlyweds. 'Pie' described his third wife as a 'grand un' but added that he had only known her three weeks.

On one occasion, after making a trip to London to attend an enquiry about a railway project, he prepared a lecture on life in the capital for the folk of his hometown. It drew large audiences at Keighley, where he delivered it in the vernacular, making it almost unintelligible to anyone not from Yorkshire. His listeners gave gasps of amazement when he stated that Londoners in high society often had fresh salmon for breakfast.

His tombstone was actually erected over his grave in 1887, which was six years before his death. The burial chamber and coffin were prepared at the same time. Unfortunately, neither the undertaker nor himself wanted to store the coffin, and for a time the problem went

'Pie' Leach's gravestone.

unsolved until a novel solution was found. He applied to store the empty coffin in the burial chamber, and the Burial Board allowed this on the provision that the usual fee for opening and closing a grave was paid. The empty coffin remained in the grave until it was needed in 1893, when 'Pie' Leach eventually passed away.

EAST RIDDLESDEN HALL

Now owned by the National Trust, East Riddlesden Hall was built in 1642 by James Murgatroyd, a wealthy clothier from Halifax. The hall was built on a small plateau overlooking a bend in the River Aire as it flows downstream from Keighley. James Murgatroyd was a Royalist, and there are many Royalist symbols and items of graffiti throughout the building. The Murgatroyd family of the 17th century had a reputation for their profanity and debauchery, with members of the family being fined, imprisoned and excommunicated. It is claimed that the Murgatroyds of East Riddlesden Hall were the inspiration of the Murgatroyd baronets in Gilbert & Sullivan's *Ruddigore*.

Standing in the grounds can be found a magnificent mediaeval tithe-barn that has survived for at least 400 years. East Riddlesden Hall is a truly remarkable house, which is reputed to be the home to a number of ghosts. Today the hall and its stunning grounds are used for private functions, such as wedding parties. In 1992 it was used a filming location for Emily Brontë's *Wuthering Heights* starring Ralph Fiennes as Heathcliffe and Juliette Binoche as Catherine. It has also been used for a number of TV productions.

ST IVES

Originally called Harden Grange, by the 19th century the estate had become known as St Ives. In the 12th and 13th centuries Halton village and Harden wood became the property of Rievaulx Abbey through a series of grants. The monks set up a 'grange' as a collecting centre for their produce. It is thought that its name is derived from a holy well that was dedicated to the seventh-century abbess St Iva. In early 17th century Harden Grange was bought and rebuilt by Robert Ferrand, a cloth merchant. Harden Hall (now St Ives) was built in 1616 and was

The 400-year-old mediaeval tithe-barn at East Riddlesden Hall.

used as a base for General Fairfax during the Civil War. In the house there was a table inscribed: 'This table was at Harden Hall when the troops under General Fairfax were encamped at Harden Moor MDCXLII'.

It is known that the history of the area goes much further back, as archaeological evidence will attest. In 1818 remains of pre-historic human activities were unearthed, and these included weapons such as spearheads, arrowheads and stone hammers, and domestic utensils, for example scrapers for preparing skins. Other finds included remains of elephant, hippopotamus and a small lion, which points to the fact that the climate must have been much hotter at that period in time. Nearby can be found the romantically named area of land called Druid's Altar, which is a rugged outcrop of millstone grit overlooking the Aire Valley. The top of the rock has a number of examples of Bronze Age cup and ring markings. Whether it was ever a place of worship as its name suggests we will perhaps never know, but it is certainly a place of inspiration. In 1844 Disraeli addressed a meeting of Young

Memorial to Mr Busfield Ferrand.

Conservatives here, and it was later to appear in his novel *Sybil*.

Near the moor stands a granite obelisk, a memorial to Mr Busfield Ferrand (1809–1889) erected by his widow, Fanny Mary Stuart,

Lady Blantyre's Rock – her son-in-law, Mr Busfield Ferrand, dedicated this rustic monument to her memory.

Stocks and Bingley Butter Cross – Bingley was granted its first market charter in 1212 by King John, and it is thought that the Butter Cross dates from that time. In 1888 it was moved from its position in the main street to Prince of Wales Park, where it stayed until 1984 when the Bingley Civic Trust prepared plans to move it back into the centre of Bingley, where it belongs.

daughter of Lord Blantyre. Busfield was a Member of Parliament who had played an active part in getting the Ten Hours Factory Bill passed. He was also a magistrate for 50 years, and for a great proportion of that time he was Chairman of the Keighley Petty Sessional Division. The St Ives estate was a favourite place with his mother-in-law, Lady Blantyre, and close to the monument can be found 'Lady Blantyre's Rock' where she used to like to sit and read. With stunning woodlands and breathtaking views across the moorland, St Ives is a delightful place and has several walks for the visitor to enjoy.

BINGLEY

A town of great antiquity, a certain Keon, brother of Egbert, Archbishop of York, spoke very highly of Bingley in 738. By 1212 the town had been granted a charter by King John to hold a market. Originally the town was founded at a ford on the River Aire, but eventually Beckfoot Bridge was constructed. This was a packhorse bridge, which was just wide enough for a single horse to cross. Later, the larger Ireland Bridge was built further upstream. This was able to accommodate more traffic and consequently soon became the main route between Bingley and the surrounding villages. When the waters of the River Aire are low a set of stepping stones can be seen. The stones could have been placed there as far back as 1,000 years. During mediaeval times Bingley was a manor that covered a considerable area in the Aire valley.

The Old White Horse Inn is one of the oldest buildings in Bingley, being a coaching house – it is located near Ireland Bridge. This Grade II listed building still has many coaching house features, such as stables and a barn. There is evidence that there has been a hostelry on this site since 1379. The Order of the Knights of St John of Jerusalem (The Knights Hospitaller) were former owners of the inn, as can be seen by the stone lanterns found on each side of the gable. Bingley appears on a 16th-century map as a single street with about 20 houses on each side. At the west end of the street stands the church, with a large house opposite, possibly the manor house. This map was produced by the cartographer Christopher Saxton, born around 1540 at Dewsbury.

On 21 March 1774 the Five Rise Locks at Bingley was opened along with a stretch of the Leeds Liverpool canal. It was a major achievement in engineering, and 30,000 people turned out to the opening. It was described in a newspaper called the *Leeds Intelligencer* as 'From Bingley to about 3 miles downwards the noblest works of the kind are exhibited viz: A fivefold, a threefold and a single lock, making

The Old White Horse at Bingley.

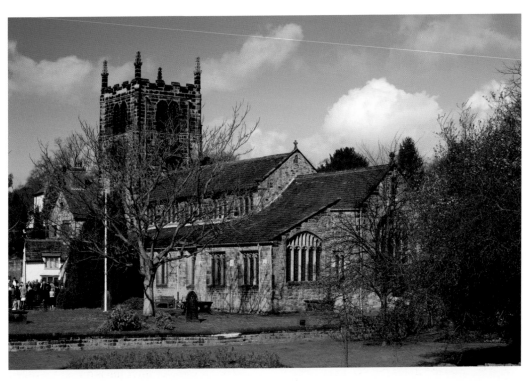

Bingley Parish Church.

together a fall of 120ft; a large aqueduct bridge of seven arches over the River Aire and an aqueduct and banking over the Shipley valley…This joyful and much wished-for event was welcomed with the ringing of Bingley bells, a band of music, the firing of guns by the neighbouring militia, the shouts of spectators, and all the marks of satisfaction that so important an acquisition merits'. It took only 28 minutes for the first boat to travel through the locks.

QUEENSBURY

It is said that it snows in June in the Bradford village of Queensbury, and it is certainly true that at a height of 1,100ft above sea level it appears to have a climate of its very own. The people of Queensbury can also lay claim to having the highest high-school in England, and it is on record that the parish church has the highest peal of bells in the British Isles. Queensbury is also famous for its brass band – The Black Dyke Band. Originally known as the 'Queenshead Band', it was formed by John Foster in 1816 at the Old Dolphin, but it was

not successful and in 1855 Foster, along with a number of other musicians, formed a new mill band named after the mill that he owned. They were outfitted with uniforms made from cloth that had been manufactured at the mill. The band has enjoyed over 150 years of success and is still one of the best-known brass bands in the world.

The company that John Foster established in 1819 is still trading today and producing fine quality materials. It is still based at Black Dyke Mills, which he began building in 1835. John Foster was born in 1798, and his father was a colliery owner and farmer from Thornton in Bradford. We know little about his early days in business, other than he started manufacturing fine worsted and mohair fabric in 1819. In the same year he married Ruth Briggs, whose father was a landowner in Queensbury. It is unknown whether he received any financial help from either his father or father-in-law to start his venture, but he managed to finance his enterprise, and by 1827 he had prospered enough to build Prospect House at the crossroads in Queensbury. He would purchase

*Black Dyke
Mills.*

Victoria Hall,
Queensbury.

yarns, which he would then distribute to handloom weavers from a warehouse at the rear of Prospect House. Once the cloth was woven they would return the pieces to him, which John would sell to merchants at Bradford Piece Hall. Prior to starting construction on Black Dyke Mills in 1835 he had rented a property called Cannon Mills for the purpose of spinning. In 1834 his father-in-law had transferred a plot of land to him called Black Myres, and it was here that he was to erect his mill. It was from a farm called Black Dyke that the mill was to get its name, but that did not come into his possession until 1842. By the mid-19th century the mill was dominating the landscape. At the Great Exhibition of 1851 at the Crystal Palace he took first prize for alpaca (he had been experimenting with its usage since 1837), and he also was awarded a gold medal for his yarns.

In 1821 his first son, William, was born, and by the time the boy was 14 he was already involved with the business. William was six years older than his brother, and because of his early involvement he was to be in a dominant position in the company. In fact the company was called John Foster & Son Ltd, and it never became known as 'Sons'. William became a full partner in 1842. The company was to construct many of the buildings in and around Queensbury. In 1891 it built the Victoria Hall for the benefit of its workers and the local community. The building included a concert hall, library, billiard room and a number of other facilities. When John Foster died in 1884, William's sons took full control of the business. Today the company is now called John Foster of England Ltd and has a worldwide reputation for weaving fine fabrics such as wool, mohair, cashmere, silk, linen and cotton.

COAL MINING IN WEST YORKSHIRE

Opposite: Hoist wheel at a coal mine.

The story of coal began in the mists of time: from about 350 to 290 million years ago during the late Palaeozoic Era, was the Carboniferous Period when great forests covered the land. These forests were not made up of trees that we would be familiar with today, but were giant ferns such as the horse tail fern, which could grow to the height of more than 30m. As the giant ferns and vegetation died, they would rot into compost on the forest floors, and over time this process would be repeated many times. Eventually the compost would form peat, which through pressure over the millions of years would form carbon-rich coal. The word Carboniferous means 'carbon bearing'. Often an imprint of a ferny leaf or piece of wood can be found when coal is broken open, which gives us a clue to its origin. There are a number of different types of coal: lignite, cannel, bituminous and anthracite. Anthracite is the hardest of them and contains the greatest percentage of carbon. Most British coalfields produce either cannel or bituminous coal.

It is not known when coal was first used, but we do know that coal was being burnt as a fuel before the Romans came to Britain. There is also some evidence of early mining as flint axes have been found embedded in coal. It is highly probable that the Romans learnt about coal from the indigenous British and were to make use of it for fuel, as coal stores have been found along Hadrian's Wall. Roman pottery kilns have been discovered to the east of Leeds, which are thought to have been fired by using outcrop coal. The first simple mines were called bell pits, and evidence of them can be found in Judy Woods near Bradford. These mines were mechanised with a windlass powered by a horse. It is known that monks were to use this form of mining. Bell pits, although relatively quick and simple to construct, were dangerous as they were prone to rock-falls and collapses. A solution was required to improve safety, and this came in the form of the room and pillar mine. Initially, a bell pit was dug, and the bottom would be squared off to form a room. Another room would be dug next to it, then another and so on. The walls between the rooms were pillars of coal, which had been left standing to support the roof. This method of mining was used for many centuries, and we have evidence that it was in use as far back as the 13th century. These mines had the benefit of ventilation and would have been lit by rush dips.

The problem with room and pillar mining was the sheer wastefulness of coal as large amounts were used to create the pillars. The introduction of long wall mining in the 17th century enabled more coal to be extracted from the mines. Teams of miners worked with picks and shovels along one wall, known as the 'face', of a tunnel. The roof of the tunnel was supported with wooden timbers. The stone waste and spoil, known as 'goaf', was deposited behind the miners. Care was taken to keep a clear road through it to give the miners access to the face.

The hollow at the side of path is all that remains of a bell pit in Jagger woods.

Once an area of coal mining, now Fairburn Ings is a nature reserve.

We cannot help but marvel at the tremendous courage of the men who ventured into the bowels of the earth to extract the precious coal, braving the threat of rock fall, explosion, poisonous gasses and sudden flash floods. The tight-knit mining communities lived with the constant knowledge that at any moment disaster may strike, announced by the dreaded colliery alarm piercing the air, which brings out the miners and their families from their homes anxious to help their friends and workmates. Wives, mothers and sweethearts gather to form the pithead vigil, desperate to learn if their loved-ones are safe. The history of coal mining in West Yorkshire has been marred with many such disasters, each tragedy leaving an empty space in the communities. Because of the dangerous nature of coal mining (before World War One a miner was killed every six hours), much was done in an attempt to improve the safety of the mines. An example was the introduction of a cage in the 1830s, which ran between fixed guide rails. Prior to this both

miners and coal were wound up and down the shaft in baskets. The danger of this method was that the baskets could twist and smash against the wall of the shaft during winding. Rocks and stones could easily hit the vulnerable miners in the baskets. There was also the possibility of the miner falling from the basket to his death.

Before the introduction of the Mines and Collieries Act of 1842, women and children under the age of 10 were working down mines. The act also made it illegal for children under 15 to work the winding gear. Many of the mine owners fought hard to prevent the act being passed. Initially the act had little effect, as there was only one inspector to ensure that the law was being obeyed. The act did, however, prove that reform was possible, and it recognised for the first time that mines needed to be controlled. During the 1850s more inspectors were appointed and owners were now required to report all fatal accidents. They were also required to keep plans of their mines. It was now possible for the inspectors to investigate major accidents. From 1851 the inspectors submitted an annual report to Parliament, and these made grim reading. The collieries were required to display seven rules, which they were forced to obey, and they could also draw up special rules for themselves. If a miner broke any of the rules, they went to prison, whereas the owner was only liable to a fine.

There can be no doubt that coal was to fuel the Industrial Revolution and that the Industrial Revolution was to bring unprecedented growth to the coal industry. Not only did the Industrial Revolution have an insatiable appetite for coal to fuel the machines of industry, but new machines were developed that enabled miners to dig deeper and more efficiently into the bowels of the earth. Greater and greater became the demand for coal, and to fulfil these demands inland waterways were expanded as well as further canals opened. There was great wealth to be made from mining coal, and so to coin a 20th-century Yorkshire saying, 'where there's muck there's brass'.

Even though there was an abundance of coal, it was still an expensive commodity and a scarce one for the many working families of the early 19th century. This was especially so for the families who lived in the mill towns and villages that had no local supplies of coal. Few families could afford to store much coal, many having no cellars or outbuildings would leave it outside. This often led to people pilfering from their neighbour's coal pile when their own supply ran out. The open fire was not only their only source of warmth, but it was also where the cooking was done in many homes of the working class. Few at the time would have the luxury of ovens and would be forced to bake on a large stone called a 'bakstone' or perhaps carry their dough to a neighbour who was fortunate to own an oven. Communities were very tight-knit and there was much mutual good-will, notwithstanding the occasional gossiping and back-biting.

By the 1940s the use of coal as an energy source began to decline, as cheaper, cleaner and more convenient fuels have become more readily available. However, coal has many other uses and can be found in dyes, explosives, fertilisers, fingernail polish, food additives, insecticides, medicines and synthetic fibres. Many of the mines have now been closed, and the communities have had to look to other trades to survive. The mines that have now been closed cannot, however, be left to their own devices, and even though they are now disused they must be managed by the Coal Authority. This is to prevent them polluting the environment. Over time, the disused mine slowly fills with water as the pumping has stopped. Eventually, this water will reach such a level as to cause it to flow out to the surrounding land. This water has stood for some considerable time and would have been in contact with the iron steel works that once supported the mine. Over time this would corrode and dissolve into the water, making it rich in iron minerals. Once exposed to air, a chemical reaction occurs that forms ochre. This ochre eventually finds its way into the river beds, which chokes the river, preventing the growth of vegetation, and for this reason the Coal Authority has a programme of installing water-treatment systems at the disused mines to prevent this pollution. Another by-product of these disused mines is methane, which collects to dangerous levels. Each year, great quantities of this gas are produced, and attempts are being made to collect this gas and use it as a source of energy. So even though now many of the mines are closed their legacy lives on.

Paying tribute to West Yorkshire's long tradition of coal mining, the National Coal Mining Museum opened to the public in 1988 as the Yorkshire Mining Museum. It is located at the Caphouse Colliery near Wakefield and is thought to be the oldest coal-mine shaft that is still in use in Britain, dating as far back as 1789. Today, however, the mine shaft is used to take visitors on a tour of the mine, as by 1985 Caphouse was exhausted of coal.

THE CITY OF WAKEFIELD

Opposite: City of Wakefield.

It was during the time of the Anglo-Saxons that Wakefield first became a settlement. The first settlers were Angles from Germany and Denmark, and it is possible that they sailed up the River Calder from the North Sea. The site would have been ideal for the settlers as it was on a hill above the river but with plenty of fresh water from springs and becks, also with fertile soil and easy communication with other settlers, either by land or water. It is possible that Wakefield was originally called Wacanfeld, and it is thought that it was named after one of the early Anglo-Saxon settlers who made his home there, called Waca, and that the name was a corruption of Waca's field.

Wakefield developed around a small church where three lanes met – Westgate, Kirkgate and Northgate. Each of the lanes would have a gate that would be shut at 8 o'clock each evening to keep wild animals out. In 867 after York was captured by the Vikings the whole area came under Norse rule, and these new invaders were to split Yorkshire into three Ridings and sub-divided these Ridings into areas called Wapentakes. The population of Wakefield at that time was mainly of Danish descent, and the settlement was the centre of a Wapentake called Agbrigg. It is thought that at that time Wakefield was considered the capital of the Scandinavian West Riding. It is interesting to see the influence of the Anglo-Saxon and Norse settlers in the names in and around Wakefield, for example, -ley (Anglo-Saxon) and -thorpe (Scandinavian). In fact, this influence can be seen throughout the whole region.

After the Norman Conquest of 1066 there was fierce resistance to these new overlords, which resulted in deadly repercussions. William the Conqueror, in a bid to quell all opposition to his rule, sent his troops into the region, and many of its inhabitants were put to the sword.

This was referred to as the 'Harrying of the North', and the destruction was widespread. It could be thought of as a mediaeval 'scorched earth policy', and it is believed that as many as 150,000 people were to perish during these reprisals. Wakefield, at the time one of the richest towns in the North, was all but wiped out. So severe was the destruction that no fields were ploughed for nine years. But Wakefield's fortunes were about to change once more, as in about the year 1090 the vast Manor of Wakefield was granted to the Earls Warenne.

According to John Leland, the 16th-century writer and antiquarian, Wakefield was, 'a very quik market toune and meately large'. He went on to say that, 'al the hole profitt of the toune standith by course drapery'. Daniel Defoe speaks of Wakefield as being clean, large, handsome and very rich. At this time its population was larger than York, and before the rise of Bradford and Leeds it was the centre of the cloth trade in Yorkshire. Other trades that brought prosperity to Wakefield were grain, coal-mining, brewing, rope-making and boat building. There is still a row of elegant Georgian houses, constructed in the 1790s, in an area called St John's, that were built with the wealth gained through grain. Wakefield was never to become an industrial centre on the scale of Bradford and Leeds, and consequently it lacks the architectural interest that some of its

A row of elegant Georgian houses in the St John's Square; developed by John Lee (1759–1836), he was a lawyer and entrepreneur, who initiated what is thought to be the first public railway – the Lake Lock Railroad.

This stunning oriel window can be found on St John's North. It is the only example on the terrace.

the throne to Robert Curthose, the king's elder brother. Before long, most of the Norman barons in England rose up in revolt against William Rufus. With the aid of a few barons, who were to remain loyal, and the English he managed to defeat the rebels. William de Warenne, one of loyal barons, was instrumental in quashing the revolt and protecting the throne and went to receive the Manor of Wakefield for his faithfulness. However, he died within a few months from a leg wound he had received at the siege of Pevensey and was succeeded by his son who was also called William.

SANDAL CASTLE

In 1106 the second earl built a motte and bailey fortress at Sandal, as a place to stay while visiting his lands in Wakefield, which he was to do no more than once or twice each year. The motte and bailey, although crude compared to the stone structure that was eventually constructed on this site, would have provided ample protection for the earl and his livestock during his brief visits. It was not until 1180 that a stone castle was to be constructed here. This was built by Hamelin Plantagenet who was the husband of Isabel de Warenne (the daughter of Earl William de Warenne III). The castle continued to be developed over the next century. Apart from a 10-year period after 1317, when the castle was captured by Thomas Earl of Lancaster, the castle was owned by the de Warenne family for well over 250 years.

It appears that from 1361 there were no further major developments that took place at Sandal Castle; this was largely due to a change of ownership. From that year the castle was in the hands of the royal family, who proved to be absentee landlords, and Sandal Castle fell into disrepair. However, in around 1484 Richard III, keen to make Sandal Castle a base for a permanent household, ordered extensive building work. Unfortunately, his plans were brought to an untimely end with his death on the

neighbours possess. This, however, is to be offset against the more open feeling that Wakefield enjoys, with many of the houses in the immediate proximity of the town centre still having private gardens.

THE MANOR OF WAKEFIELD AND THE EARLS OF WARENNE

The first earl, William de Warenne, had been one of William the Conqueror's chief men during the invasion of 1066. After the invasion he was rewarded with the grant of about 300 manors scattered over 12 counties and was created Earl of Surrey. His principal castle was at Lewes in Sussex. After the death of William the Conqueror (also known as William the Bastard) in 1087, his favourite son William Rufus was crowned King of England. After his coronation on 29 September 1087, it soon became apparent that not all was well when a number of barons refused to attend the following Easter court and had in fact offered

The remains of Sandal Castle.

field of Bosworth in 1485. Richard was the last King of England to die on the battlefield, and his death brought an end to the Wars of the Roses. Interestingly, his father Richard, the Duke of York, was slain 25 years earlier at the Battle of Wakefield. The battle was fought under the shadow of Sandal Castle on 30 December 1460 and is said to be the origins of the nursery rhyme *The Grand Old Duke of York*.

Over time, Sandal Castle was allowed to fall into decay, and many parts of the castle became uninhabitable, as buildings had missing floors and even missing roofs in some cases. There is evidence, however, that some of the buildings near the main drawbridge remained occupied and were used as dwellings by the constable of the castle. It was not until 1645 and the English Civil War that it once again saw active service. The castle was re-fortified and used as a garrison by the Royalists; their occupation was to be short-lived, and on 1 October 1645 the garrison

surrendered to the Parliamentarian forces. On orders of Parliament, the castle was destroyed and left to become overgrown. It was only during recent excavations between 1964 and 1973 that the true extent of the surviving stonework was revealed. Today, as the visitor stands at the top of the mound where the keep once stood and looks over the green and peaceful fields, it is hard to imagine that they were once the scenes of dreadful carnage and bloodshed.

THE BATTLE OF WAKEFIELD

On the morning of 28 December 1460, the Lancastrian forces left Pontefract Castle and marched towards the Yorkists who were gathered at Sandal Castle. It was a nine-mile march, and their route took them across the high ground. The Lancastrian force is thought to have been about 15,000 men and, although their approach would have been reasonably hidden from the castle, there is no doubt that the Duke of York

Standing on top of Sandal Castle looking over the fields towards the City of Wakefield, it is hard to imagine that it was the scene of so much bloodshed so many centuries ago.

was well aware of their presence, for his scouts would have kept him informed of their progress. Many of the Yorkists took refuge in the castle; however, the size of the force meant that many would be forced to take up their positions on the flat ground in front of it.

Before long, the Lancastrian forces were positioning themselves on both sides and preparing to do battle. The Lancastrians brought no siege equipment with them, and they were very aware that if they were unable to draw the Duke out of his castle there was every danger that he would sit tight and wait for reinforcements to arrive. In an attempt to draw him out and into battle they began to taunt him. We have no record of what the taunts were, but whatever they were they did the trick, and the Duke left his stronghold. On 30 December 1460 battle commenced. The slaughter was frightful, and many hundreds perished. With his back to a willow tree, the Duke of York fell fighting to the last. He refused requests to yield and preferred to die fighting than live a life of ignominy. On the spot where the Duke had fallen was found a ring, which appeared to be of great antiquity, and

upon it were engraved the following words 'Pour bon amour' meaning 'For good love'. The ring also had the effigies of Christ, the Virgin Mary, and two other saints. Sadly, the ring has long since disappeared. The Lancastrian forces hacked off the great Duke's head and impaled it on the gates of York for all to see, placing a paper crown on top of it.

ST MARY'S CHANTRY CHAPEL

On the outskirts of the City of Wakefield is old Wakefield Bridge on which we find St Mary's Chantry Chapel. This quaint chapel was built in the middle of the bridge in 1360 as a resting

St Mary's Chantry Chapel.

place for travellers. There were only six of these bridge chapels built in Britain, of which four remain today. The bridge played another vital role for Wakefield, as it was an important crossing place over the river, and travellers had to pay for the privilege of using it.

It was also the site of a cruel and dreadful event. After the Battle of Wakefield in 1460, Edmund, the 17-year-old Earl of Rutland, was fleeing from the battlefield, along with his tutor and protector; his father Richard the Duke of York had been slain on the field of battle. It is possible that Edmund was attempting to reach the sanctuary of the chapel, but almost at its door he was captured by Lord Clifford. At first Clifford had not realised who his captive was, but as the boy's true identity dawned on him he flew into a rage and butchered Edmund with his dagger, exclaiming, 'By God's blood, thy father slew mine; and so will I do thee, and all thy kin.' In what was possibly poetic justice, Lord Clifford was to be killed a few months later, trying to escape from the battlefield at Ferrybridge.

Today the chapel is no longer a sanctuary for the weary traveller, and the bridge has now been by-passed by a larger, wider and more modern structure across the River Calder. During the mid-19th century the frontage of the chantry had become in such a sorry state of disrepair that Sir Gilbert Scott was commissioned to examine the building and to advise on what could be done. His recommendation was to completely replace it, and this was done in 1847 with an exact copy of the original one. The old façade, however, was not scrapped but used for a combined boat and summerhouse beside the lake in the grounds of Kettlethorpe Hall.

Unfortunately, in using soft stone to make the replacement, it was not long before that too had seriously deteriorated. By 1940 it became necessary to replace the façade for a third time. This was done despite shortages of materials and manpower caused by the hostilities of World War Two. The chantry has served a number of uses apart from being a place of worship. It has been a tailor's shop, a library, an old clothes shop and a warehouse. It was once also used to house a large water cistern, preventing the surrounding area being spoilt with the unsightly object. Today this historic building is once more used for the purpose it was intended, and services now take place on the first Sunday of each month.

CATHEDRAL OF ALL SAINTS

A church lay at the centre of the Anglo-Saxon settlement, which had been dedicated to All Hallows (All Saints). It is possible that the site that the church was built on was originally pagan sacred ground. It was common practice to build churches on land that would have already been considered consecrated, as it made it easier to convert the populace to Christianity. In about 1100 the church was rebuilt in the Norman style, with its typical central tower and the body of the church in the shape of cross. Over the years, as the local population grew, many alterations and

The spire of Wakefield Cathedral towers over all the surrounding buildings.

additions were made to it, but unfortunately these structural alterations weakened the building until eventually in 1315 the central tower collapsed, destroying part of the building. The church was rebuilt, and it was decided to make it larger, wider and taller, but without the central tower. A new tower and spire was built at the west end of the church, which was completed in 1420. This spire is the tallest in Yorkshire, being 247ft high. As with many churches, this building suffered badly during the English Civil War when it lost its font and organ. General neglect over the following centuries was to leave the church in a poor state of repair. It was not until about the 1860s that major renovations took place under the direction of Sir George Gilbert Scott. The interior of the church was given a makeover to give it a more mediaeval look, and the spire was rebuilt. In 1888 the church was chosen from a shortlist to become a cathedral, and among the rivals that it beat off were St Mary's at Mirfield and St John's at Halifax, both outstanding buildings. Wakefield was now designated a city. Even today, the spire offers an impressive sight as it towers over the other buildings below and is a readily recognisable landmark on the horizon.

ST JOHN'S CHURCH

Constructed in 1795 by Charles Watson, the beautiful church of St John's was built in the centre of a Georgian square of the same name. The church was to be the crowning glory of a Georgian town planning scheme that sadly was never completed. The church is unmistakeably Georgian in design and has many interesting features. The tower possesses a delightful octagonal top-stage, complete with domed cap and a pedimented Tuscan doorway. Additions were added in 1905 from designs by F.T. Micklethwaite.

WALTON HALL

Adventurer, explorer and true English eccentric, Charles Waterton (1782–1865) may have labelled himself as 'the most commonplace of men', but fighting snakes, riding alligators and living like a monk is certainly not what most people would describe as commonplace, nor even normal. Renowned for his extensive travels, natural history observations and prolific writings, Charles Waterton was a man ahead of his time, turning his family estate into a nature reserve, which he opened to the general public. His book *Wanderings in South America* has never been out of print since first published in 1825, although his writings could have a darker side as he was formidable satirist and pamphleteer. Charles Waterton could have been the inspiration for Lewis Carroll's Mad Hatter: he was a devotee of that most English form of humour – the practical joke. He would dress as a dog and bite the legs of visitors who approached his front door.

As an adventurer travelling through South America he had prepared a speech to introduce himself to the natives: 'Ladies and Gentlemen, I come to see you and admire your beautiful country, not to eat you nor be eaten by you'. Among his essentials for his travels were an umbrella, flannel underwear as a 'great preserver of health in the hot countries and tea – warm and weak and plenty of it'. Charles Waterton was from an illustrious lineage – his paternal grandmother Mary More was descended from

The delightful Georgian-designed church of St John's.

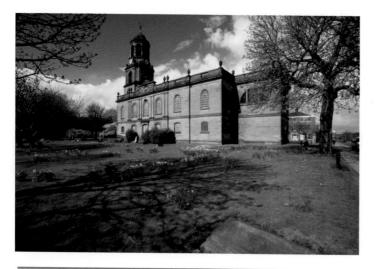

Walton Hall in the evening light.

Sir Thomas More, the famous writer, statesman and philosopher. The Waterton family name is linked with the village of Walton as far back as 1435, when a certain Richard Waterton commissioned the building of Walton Hall on his marriage. This mediaeval hall survived the rigours of time and even the cannonballs of the Parliamentarians. It is said that the lady of the hall lead the defending forces under siege and was narrowly missed by a musket ball shot by Oliver Cromwell himself. Sadly, the original hall was demolished by Thomas Waterton in 1767 and replaced with the present building. All that remains of the first hall is a ruined water gate.

In 1829 Charles Waterton married the daughter of an old friend; he was 47 and she was just 17. Tragically, she was to die 12 months later during childbirth; however, the child survived – a boy. Charles blamed himself for her death, and from that moment until he died in 1865 he was to live a life of penance. He was to never again sleep in a bed but wrapped himself in a blanket with a block of wood as a pillow and slept on the bare floorboards. Each night at midnight he would spend a few minutes in the chapel, then at 3.30am he would get up and spend an hour in prayer. Apart from his well-known eccentricities, his other more enduring legacies would be his additions to the pool of human knowledge with his scientific writings on fauna and especially the bird life of the South American continent. In fact, his work was much valued by Charles Darwin, who visited him at Walton Hall. But perhaps the last words should be left to his friend Thackeray

The ruined water gate.

St Peter's at Horbury, designed and built by John Carr as a gift to his birthplace.

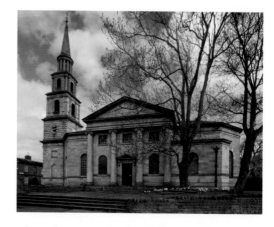

who wrote 'I could not but feel a kindness and admiration for the good man. I know his works are made to square with his faith; that he dines on a crust, lives as chastely as a hermit, and gives his all to the poor.'

HORBURY

Although Horbury has a town hall, which was built in 1902, strictly speaking it is not a town as it has never received a charter from the Crown, nor did it declare itself a town under the post-1974 rules. Horbury is a picturesque and tranquil place with a number of interesting period buildings, including the remains of Horbury Hall, a timber-framed mediaeval property. Walking through the pleasant streets of Horbury, admiring the many examples of fine architecture, it is difficult to imagine that it is also a centre for heavy industry. During World War Two the local firm of Charles Roberts, an engineering company specialising in railways, built Churchill tanks. They are also credited with producing the millionth bomb of the war. It was at Horbury that the Luddites were to achieve their greatest act of damage,

when they completely destroyed Fosters Mill, which was located near the River Calder. This act of vandalism was a result of desperation and fear that the machines would deprive the weavers from making a living.

Horbury is also the birthplace of the famous 18th-century architect, John Carr. Born in 1723, he was the eldest of nine children. His father was a master mason, and it was through him that he received his training. In 1748 he left his father's employment to start an independent career, which he continued until shortly before his death in 1807. His output of work was truly staggering, including public buildings, churches,

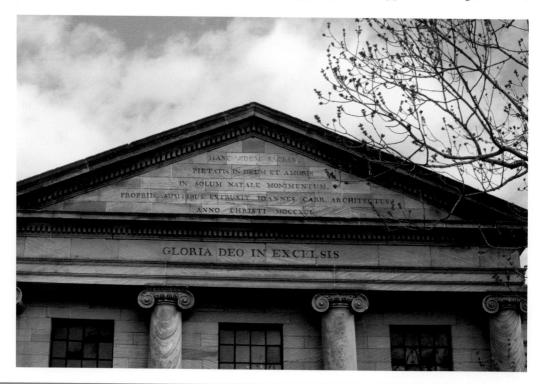

Latin inscription over entrance of St Peter's.

Tithe Barn Street.

bridges and many private homes such as Harewood House. Although many of his commissions were in his native Yorkshire, he undertook work further afield, and one of his largest projects, which was only partially finished, was the St Antonio Hospital in Portugal. John Carr was greatly influenced by the 16th-century Italian architects Sebastiano Serlio and Andrea Palladio. Throughout his career he was to witness a number of major changes in architectural styles. John's early work could be described as a mixture of Palladian and Rococo, and during the middle period of his work he sought the more pure lines of Antique Roman style with French influences. At the end of his career he returned to the Palladian style of his youth. Many of his buildings can still be seen

today. He also designed, built and paid for a church in his birthplace; dedicated to St Peter. It was built in 1793 and cost £8,000 to construct. John Carr died on 22 February 1807 and is buried in his church at Horbury. Above the main entrance of this stunning edifice is carved a Latin inscription describing his association with the town.

Horbury is also known as the home of the hymn *Onward, Christian Soldiers*, written by the Reverend Sabine Baring-Gould (1834–1924) for the children to sing as they marched to church at Whitsuntide in 1865. Opening in 1858, the Victorian House of Mercy was founded to rescue fallen women from sin and destitution. Developing into a huge complex of a convent, chapel, hospital and a retreat for clergy, it was subsequently renamed St Peter's convent. In 1949 it opened as a private preparatory school named St Hilda, which is still going strong today.

THE PROPHET WROE

Described by the *Free Press* on 28 February 1874 as 'a man of peculiar appearance who inspired uneducated and wonder-loving people with a strange fascination', John Wroe was born in 1782 at Bowling near Bradford. After receiving little education, he began work for his father, who was a worsted manufacturer and farmer. Later he was to start his own farm, marry and bring up three children. It was at the age of 37 that his life would completely change. Contracting a life-threatening fever and fearing that he would not recover, Wroe became seriously concerned with his own spiritual well-being. The fever passed, however, and he appeared to make a miraculous recovery. After his recovery he began to experience visions or trances, and it was during these trances that remarkable events were revealed to him. In 1820 he joined the Southcottians in Leeds. The Southcottians, also known as the Christian Israelites, followed the teachings of Joanna

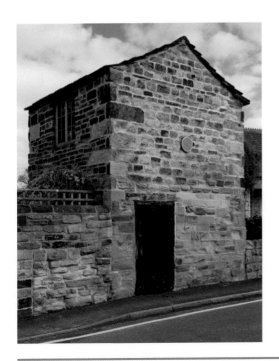

The kidcote – once Horbury's lock-up, where a lawbreaker could expect to end up for a spell.

Southcott (1750–1814) a self-professed religious prophetess from Gittisham, Devon.

Within two years John Wroe was their leader, and in 1824 while being baptised in front of a crowd that was reputed to be around 30,000 he announced that he would part the waters of the River Aire and walk across. This, he proclaimed, would be a sign of his divine authority. The waters failed to do his bidding, but this failure strangely did little to dent his credibility with his followers. In the same year he was publicly circumcised. Wroe announced that in a vision he 'had a command from heaven to take seven virgins to cherish and comfort him.' The girls were found from the daughters of three families, and Wroe set off on a preaching tour with them. A scandal broke out, however, when he returned and one of them was found to be pregnant. Indignant at this, some of his followers attempted to hold an inquiry, which broke down into a shambles as fighting broke out and pews, fittings, doors and windows were broken. Wroe managed to convince a number of them that the unborn child was to be a Messiah, and great preparations were made for the birth. Among the preparations was the making of a wonderful cradle of blue silk and gold, which was said to have cost £200 to make (a princely sum indeed). When the child was born it was a girl. As they were expecting a boy, it rather threw a spanner in their plans and, with his followers losing patience with him, Wroe was forced to leave town.

It was then that John Wroe began a life of travel and propaganda. During the late 1840s and early 1850s he travelled extensively throughout America and Australia. He received great financial support in Australia, which partially funded the building of a great house at Wrenthorpe near Wakefield. It was while having one of his trances that God had told him to build a mansion for the Messiah to dwell. During his vision he received precise details on the design of this mansion. The final building,

however, owed more to how he remembered the design of Melbourne Town Hall. The *Free Press* described Prophet Wroe's Temple as 'Prophet Wroe's Mansion...It stands on a fine commanding eminence, which slopes gently to the south from which a view of the whole country for many miles round can be obtained. The grounds, consisting of several acres, are well ordered, and abundantly stocked with beautiful trees, and at each of the four corners there is a porter's lodge, and a carriage drive sweeping round to the south front of the hall. The forcing-houses are extensive and full of vines and various fruits from many lands. The stables furnish abundant accommodation for a numerous stud. The house itself is a fine mansion-like structure with south, east and west fronts; and the principal rooms are said to be panelled with cedar.'

John Wroe died at Fitzroy, Australia in 1864. He had promised that he would never die, and his Australian followers felt so aggrieved at being let down that they demanded their subscriptions back. On his death, Melbourne

This sculpture represents rhubarb and is to commemorate the fact that this area is in the World famous Yorkshire 'rhubarb triangle'.

House, which had purposely built for the members of the House of Israel, passed to his grandson and the community was dispersed. The new leader of the sect, an American called Daniel Milton, claimed that the house belonged to the Christian Israelites and not Wroe's relatives. For a time he led a campaign to gain rightful occupation of the house, which included pasting bills on the walls of the property. The house remained the property of the Wroe family until the 1930s. Today Melbourne House belongs to a telecommunication company.

WRENTHORPE

Four hundred years ago Wrenthorpe was the centre of a thriving pottery industry. There were a number of kilns in the centre of the village, which gave rise to term 'pot 'ole' or 'pot 'oil', which even today is still used by some of older locals when referring to the village centre. It was the availability of the raw materials that led to the growth of this industry, which for a time rivalled that of Stoke. As well as pots and

jugs, the village produced clay pipes to cater for the growing demand from tobacco smokers. From time to time clay pipes and pieces of pottery still turn up in gardens throughout the village. Unable to compete with Stoke's growing output of pottery, by the end of the 1780s the industry in Wrenthorpe had all but died out.

During open-cast mining in the 1980s, bell pits from former times were discovered. These primitive mines dating back to mediaeval times give clear evidence that the coal mining industry had flourished there for many hundreds of years. Wrenthorpe also had a thriving rope industry, which began in the early 19th century. Ropes are no longer made at the village, but several houses built by the owners of rope works are still standing. These rope works were known as 'rope walks', and to this day there is a local footpath known as the 'band walk'. Rope made at Wrenthorpe was used for many purposes, including to tie up great ocean-going liners and even the hangman's noose.

Wrenthorpe was the location of the first red-brick building to be built in the Wakefield area. Red Hall was constructed in around 1610 and was built on the site of a large Tudor mansion. Today, Wrenthorpe is still a relatively small village with a population of 6,000 and has a large conservation area on its southern edge, called the Alverthorpe and Wrenthorpe Meadows.

NOSTELL PRIORY

This stunning 18th-century building was constructed on the site of a mediaeval priory that had been dedicated to St Oswald. Friars had occupied the site from when the priory had been first founded in the 12th century until the Dissolution of the Monasteries by Henry VIII in the 16th century. Over the years, the buildings and land passed through a number of hands until in 1654 it was bought by Rowland Winn, a London Alderman. The construction of the stately home was started in 1733 by Sir Rowland

A monument to Wrenthorpe's pottery past.

The stupendous Nostell Priory.

Winn and the architect James Paine (who was only 19 when he commenced on the project). The building was constructed to the north of the old priory and took about 50 years to complete. They spent eight years designing and building the central part of the home but had planned to produce a larger house. The building had been constructed in the Palladian style that was very popular at the time and had been named after the Italian architect Andrea Palladio (1508–1580).

Unfortunately, they did not finish their plans. When Sir Rowland died in 1765, it was left to his son, who was also called Sir Rowland, to complete the building. He employed the services of Robert Adam to finish the house. Robert designed extensions for both sides of the house in the Neo-Classical style, but only the north wing was added. He also designed the front terrace and stable block. He was responsible for many of the room's interiors, and his elegant classic designs contrast with the flamboyant rococo designs of James Paine.

Nostell Priory is notable for its outstanding art collections – it holds the biggest collection of Thomas Chippendale furniture in the country. In fact almost every room has an example of the famous furniture-maker's work. The house also has tapestries by Van der Borcht and paintings by Van Dyck, Holbein and Hogarth. In 1885 Sir Rowland was given the title Lord St Oswald after the patron saint of the mediaeval priory. Although in 1953 the priory, complete with its contents, was given to the National Trust, it still remains the family home for the present Lord and Lady St Oswald. Very little of the building has changed since it was first built, and with its 300 acres of parkland Nostell Priory is certainly a jewel in our wonderful heritage and a national treasure to be rightly proud of.

DAME MARY BOLLES' WATER TOWER

Below the village of Heath stands a tower called Dame Mary Bolles' Water Tower. It was built in the 17th century over a hillside spring. The spring water was used to power a water wheel that would pump water up to the now ruined Old Heath Hall, which stood on the hill above.

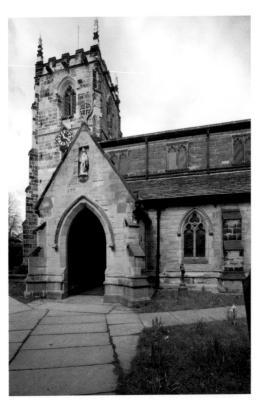

Far left: Dame Mary Bolles' water tower.

St Cuthbert's at Ackworth.

It is reputed that Dame Mary practised in the dark arts of witchcraft and that she requested that the room that died in was to be sealed. When she died in 1662 the room in the Old Hall was sealed as she had asked, but legend has it that when the room was unsealed 50 years later her ghost appeared and proceeded to haunt the surrounding area.

The village of Heath is made up of about 20 properties; mainly substantial 18th-century villas that had been designed by James Paine and John Carr, two respected architects of their time. Today Heath is a much sought after village that was once called 'the village of mansions'.

ACKWORTH ALMSHOUSES
The village of Ackworth was originally an Anglo-Saxon settlement in around the year 500. The settlement had been made from clearing oak trees to form an enclosure and hence its name – Ack (oak) Worth (enclosure). There is a local tradition that maintains that the body of St Cuthbert was brought to Ackworth by the

monks of Lindisfarne as they escaped the ravages of the Vikings. This tradition is celebrated in the dedication of the church of St Cuthbert's in Ackworth.

In 1666 two almshouses were founded by the local Rector Thomas Bradley. Although not a Yorkshireman himself, his grandfather had been. Thomas Bradley was loyal to the king, and during the siege of Pontefract in 1644 he was a preacher to the Royalist troops. In 1645 the

Ackworth village cross – Cromwell's troops knocked off the cross because they considered it a symbol of 'popery' and replaced it with the puritanical sphere.

111

Parliamentarians occupied Ackworth, and he was deprived of his living. He suffered greatly during the Interregnum, which was the period after the execution of Charles I and ended with the Restoration of the Monarchy with Charles II, a period of 11 years. Thomas Bradley attended Charles I at his execution. He resigned in 1672, and he died the following year on 10 October 1673.

ACKWORTH SCHOOL

Founded in 1779, Ackworth School is one of the older schools in Britain. It was established by John Fothergill for Quaker boys and girls and run with a Quaker Christian ethos. Although it is still a Quaker school, it is no longer only opened to just Quakers, and nowadays the majority of the pupils come from non-Quaker families; however, pupils are still expected to attend a Quaker meeting each morning to reflect and spend some time in silence.

ACKWORTH PLAGUE STONE

In 1645 there was an outbreak of bubonic plague, which claimed the lives of 153 villagers.

On Castle Syke Hill there can be found a plague stone that dates from this period. The villagers would get supplies from out of the village by leaving coins in a hollow in the top of the stone.

Ackworth Quaker's school.

112

So as not to pass on the deadly disease they would fill the hollow with a disinfectant such as vinegar and therefore purify the coins. Food would then be left for the villagers to collect. It is said that the bodies of the plague victims were buried in a field called 'Burial Field'. This place had also been the scene of some fierce fighting between the Royalists and Parliamentarian forces earlier in the same year, so presumably this field had already been used as a mass burial site.

This was not the first time that Ackworth had been visited by this evil scourge, as it had also fallen victim during the late 1340s, when the great pandemic called the Black Death wiped out around a third of the population. It is unknown how many were to die in Ackworth, but assuming the death toll was similar to other towns and villages throughout the country then we can surmise that about 30 per cent of its inhabitants would have perished. There are three forms of plague: bubonic, pneumonic and septicemic. However the most common form during the Black Death was bubonic, so called because of the enlarged lymphatic gland or bubo, which would appear on the neck, armpits or groin. The bubonic plague still exists in the world today; however, we can now cure it as long as it is dealt with quickly. Meanwhile the 'Plague Stone' at Ackworth acts as a reminder as to how terrible this disease once was and how feared among the populace.

FERRYBRIDGE

At the crossing point of the Great North Road, a bridge was built over the River Aire in 1198. It can be assumed, however, that a form of crossing predates that bridge as Ferrybridge possesses one of the oldest archaeological features in the region – The Ferrybridge Henge. This prehistoric ceremonial monument dates back to Neolithic times and was built between 4500 and 1500BC. Recent excavation has unearthed a chariot burial dating back 2,400

Ferrybridge – designed by John Carr and built by Bernard Hartley.

years. Previously, a sword and scabbard believed to be Iron Age had been discovered at this important site. The sword had been deliberately bent and broken, which is thought to have been a common practice when making ceremonial offerings. The scabbard is now displayed in the British Museum. It was during mediaeval times that the site lost its significance as a sacred place. Sadly, during the 19th century idle curiosity and the thought of hidden treasure did much to damage the site. Further damage and loss of important relics of our past was done when the Ferrybridge 'C' Powerstation was built.

This was once a toll bridge, and the toll house can be seen in the background.

At the end of the 14th century the bridge over the River Aire was replaced with a bridge with seven pillars and a chantry chapel at one end. A toll was required to cross the bridge until the early 19th century. The chantry chapel is no longer there, and the stone bridge that now spans the River Aire was designed by John Carr in 1797. The bridge was completed seven years later by the Pontefract builder, Bernard Hartley. Today the bridge no longer carries traffic travelling north and has been superseded by a motorway fly-over. The old toll house still remains standing almost in the shadow of the Ferry bridge 'C' Powerstation, its enormous cooling towers looming over the surrounding landscape.

On 27 March 1461 an engagement took place between the forces of the House of Lancaster and those of the House of York. This was to become called the Battle of Ferrybridge, which was a prelude to the carnage that was to follow two days later at Towton, considered the bloodiest battle ever to be fought in England. It is said that the cost in life at Ferrybridge was high, and it is thought that as many as 3,000 were slaughtered, with many to perish either in the freezing waters of the river or by the withering hail of arrows. We tend to think of the Middle Ages as a time of knights, damsels and chivalry. In reality the battles were bloody affairs that were cruel and inhumane, and loss of life was heavy; especially among the common men as there would be no question of sparing their lives.

In 1530 Cardinal Wolsey had travelled to Yorkshire, having been made Archbishop of York 16 years earlier, but this was the first time he had visited the county. He was out of favour with Henry VIII after failing to secure the king's divorce, and there was no doubt that after making many enemies throughout his career there were many who were ready to take full advantage of his fall from grace. He was charged with treason and ordered back to London so, accompanied by his personal chaplain Edmund Bonner, they set off for the capital. Although he was suffering great distress, he found the opportunity while on the journey to confirm some 200 children on the Green at Ferrybridge. By this time he was seriously ill and was never to reach his destination of the Tower of London as he died at Leicester on 29 November 1530.

SIR MARTIN FROBISHER

It is thought that Sir Martin Frobisher was born in Altofts, a village near Normanton, in 1539. He lost his father at an early age and was sent to school in London and placed under the care of a relative, Sir John York. It was this guardian who was to set him on his career by placing him on board a merchant ship that, along with a small fleet of others, was bound for Guinea. While in Guinea he was captured by a native chief and held prison by the Portuguese. For the next 15 years he sailed the seas as a pirate plundering the Spanish ships. Although he brought home much booty, he never became rich through the spoils, but it did make him extremely unpopular with the Spanish.

In the early 1560s he became fascinated with the idea of finding the North-West Passage to China. Three times he attempted the perilous journey through the polar ice packs but to no avail. On one of his failed attempts he brought back many tonnes of black ore, which was rumoured to be gold but turned out to be worthless. Although he was a brave sailor he never achieved any real financial success from his adventures. In 1588 he commanded the famous *Triumph* during the defeat of the Spanish Armada, serving beside Sir Francis Drake whom he detested. Distinguishing himself during the battle, he was later knighted by Elizabeth I as a result of his great service in the dispersion of the Spanish Fleet.

Although he owned two extensive estates, one at Finningley Grange in Nottinghamshire and the other was the Manor of Whitwood in West Yorkshire, his adventures at sea meant that he was unable to spend much time enjoying them. After the Armada he spent the next few years harrying the Spanish ships off the coast of Spain. It was during a mission to help French Huguenots under siege at Crozon in Brittany that he was to be wounded by Spanish chain shot and died a few days later from bungled surgery. His body was buried at St Giles-without-Cripplegate in London, while his internal organs were buried in St Andrew's in Plymouth. His widow was to marry John Savile of the Yorkshire house of that name.

PONTEFRACT, THE CASTLE AND POMFRET CAKES

Between 1066 and 1400 the largest town in West Yorkshire was neither Leeds nor Bradford, that honour went to Pontefract. The importance of Pontefract was due to its castle with its large garrison. The large number of troops encouraged a wide range of traders to Pontefract to cater for their needs. The castle was also popular with visiting monarchs and the nobility whose presence also increased the growth of the town.

Pontefract's prosperity was further increased in 1257 when it received a charter enabling it to hold a market. Another advantage that it enjoyed was its location being set in a highly productive agricultural area.

Pontefract derives its name from two Latin words: 'pons', meaning bridge, and 'fractus', meaning broken. It is thought to refer to an old Roman bridge over the River Aire that was destroyed by William I in 1069. The name Pontefract does not appear in the *Domesday Book*, but an area called Tanshelf does. The town's motto is 'Post mortem patris pro filio', a reference to Royalist sympathies in the English Civil War, and means 'After the death of the father support the son'. The famous Pontefract Castle was built during Norman times, at which time the town was called Pomfret. It was built by the lord of the manor, Ilbert de Lacy, in around 1070. The castle was the scene of many dark deeds, and it is thought that Richard II was murdered within its walls. These events were immortalised in William Shakespeare's play *Richard III*:

> Pomfret, Pomfret! O thou bloody prison,
> Fatal and ominous to noble peers!
> Within the guilty closure of thy walls
> Richard the second here was hack'd to death;
> And, for more slander to thy dismal seat,
> We give thee up our guiltless blood to drink.

The town suffered greatly through the English Civil War as the castle was a particular target for Cromwell's forces. It was said by

Far left: The ruins of Pontefract Castle.

The Ferrybridge Power Station seen from the grounds of Pontefract Castle.

The dramatic half-ruined church of All Saints.

Oliver Cromwell that the castle was one of the strongest inland garrisons in the kingdom. The castle was put under siege three times, leaving the town impoverished and the population depleted. It was after the end of the third siege on 24 March 1649 that, fearing the possibility of a fourth, the people of Pontefract petitioned Parliament for the castle to be demolished. The demolition began less than a month later. The few remains that are left standing leave us in no doubt that at its peak this castle would have been an impressive sight.

Standing almost in the shadow of the castle on the north-eastern side of the town lies the dramatic half-ruined All Saints Church. The church had been a parochial centre since Anglo-Saxon times. Much of the church that we see today lies in ruins. It was a casualty of the English Civil War and the constant struggle between the Royalists and Parliamentarians to gain supremacy of the castle and the surrounding area. During an attempt by the Parliamentarians to remove the Royalists, it is reported that a total of 60 18lb cannonballs were fired at the church. Recently, a cannonball was found still embedded

The church tower framed by the arch of a ruined window.

into one of the walls, although this cannonball was only 2in in diameter and weighed 2oz. The Parliamentarians finally occupied the church in June 1645 and proceeded to plunder it of

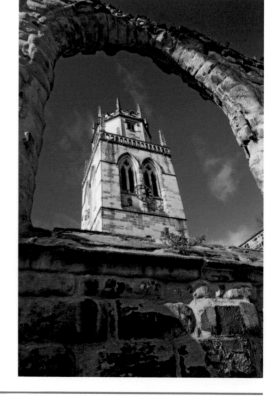

iron, wood and lead. Four years later the church was a total ruin.

It was left in this ruined state until 1838 when the architect, Robert Dennis Chantrell, built a new church in the centre of the ruins. How much repair work was undertaken on the tower is not known, but we do know that the damage was repaired and a clock face added. The tower (construction started in the early 14th century) is of interest and deserves some description. In the north-west corner of the lower part of the tower is the famous double helix staircase. This consists of two staircases which are wound around the same stone newel, like strands of DNA. The only other examples of these types of staircases can be found in St Ethilda's Church at Tamworth and Chateau de Chambard in France. At the end of the 14th century an octagon was built on top of the tall square tower, giving this church its distinctive look. Final work on the tower was completed sometime in the 15th century.

It is interesting to note that Pontefract possesses two parish churches, All Saints being the original parish church. However, after its destruction and abandonment it was essential to designate another as the parish church. This honour went to St Giles, a delightful church that was built in around 1106 in the centre of Pontefract, near to the site of St Oswald's preaching cross. In 1789 the Chapel of St Giles became the parish church of Pontefract. The church possesses a distinctive octagonal clock tower, which stands as a landmark above

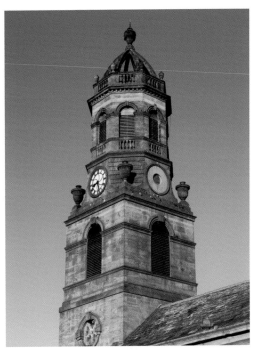

Pontefract. When All Saints was repaired in the 1830s it once again became a parish church.

Next to St Giles stands the famous Buttercross, built in 1734 to shelter people while selling their dairy products. Built on the site of St Oswald's preaching hut, this stone construction was a gift to the people of Pontefract, given posthumously by Solomon Dupeer. According to a plaque on one of the walls of the Buttercross, he was reputed to have betrayed Gibraltar to the British in 1704. As well as the Buttercross there are a number of clues to Pontefract being a market town. A quick look at some of its street names gives evidence to its past, such as Market Place, Beastfair and Shoemarket. It is documented that in 1258 there were a number of small shops or 'seldes' occupied by cobblers. These shops had developed on the site of an open market. In 1860 the Market Hall was opened by the Prime Minister, Viscount Palmerston. Designed by Joseph Wilson, the market was built on the site that had been selling fresh meat since the 14th century and since the 17th century had been known as the Shambles. Pontefract possesses an attractive inn, called the Counting House. This

Detail of door at All Saints.

The Counting House.

can be found along Swales Yard. This building was once part of the three-aisled Manor House, which had been allowed to fall into ruins. Once owned by the Mayor of Pontefract in the mid-16th century, this inn is full of character and has many fine features, such as the original oak beams.

Perhaps the one thing that Pontefract is famous for above all else is its liquorice. It is the quality of its sandy soil that makes Pontefract one of the few places in Britain that it be successfully grown. Although liquorice is no longer grown here, the famous Pontefract or Pomfret cakes are still made. The town has two liquorice factories and a Liquorice Festival is held each year. There is even a poem celebrating

Pontefract's liquorice called *The Liquorice Fields at Pontefract*, written by Poet Laureate Sir John Betjeman. Currently, there are ongoing trials to reintroduce the liquorice crop into the district.

Now housing Pontefract Museum, this stunning Art Nouveau building was once the local library. It was built as a Free Library with money donated by Andrew Carnegie. Designed by local architects, Garside and Pennington in 1904, they took their inspiration from the Art Nouveau movement, which was very much in vogue throughout Europe at that time. The graceful terracotta works outside the building with tulip motifs were typical of Art Nouveau. The library was to open with a catalogue of just over 2,000 books.

By 1935 the library had grown to nearly 13,000 books, and by the 1960s the collection of books had outgrown the building. During the 1970s the town centre was undergoing transformation, and part of this development included a new library. In 1978 the building was opened as a museum. Today this free museum offers an interesting collection of exhibits that comprehensively tell the story of Pontefract's history from prehistoric times through to today.

Far right: The graceful Art Nouveau motifs that adorn the exterior of Pontefract's Free Library (now a museum).

Pontefract's famous Pomfret cakes.

THE HIGHWAYMAN

Popular legend has it that Dick Turpin rode his horse, Black Bess, from London to York in a day. Although the story is true, it was not Dick Turpin who accomplished this feat, but a certain James Nevison (nicknamed 'Swift Nick'). It is thought that he was born near Pontefract in 1648; this notorious highwayman was considered something of a 'Robin Hood' character by many – robbing the rich to give to the poor. The truth, however, was more prosaic, as he was no more than a common criminal, albeit a charming one.

The story began one summer morning at 4am in 1676, when he robbed a traveller at Gads Hill in Kent. Making his escape on a bay mare, he crossed the River Thames by ferry. He galloped northwards, ensuring that he gave his horse regular rests. Heading towards York he reached his destination at sunset. This was an amazing achievement for both man and horse, as they had covered 200 miles in a single day. Once he arrived at York he stabled his horse at an inn, washed himself and, changing his travel-stained clothes, he then strolled to a bowling green, where he knew the lord mayor would be found. To ensure that the lord mayor remembered him, he struck up a conversation and even had a small wager with him over the outcome of a game.

He was later arrested and charged with the robbery at Gads Hill. At his trial he brought forward the lord mayor as a witness, who was able to give the highwayman an alibi and the jury, unable to believe that he could have covered that distance in a day, acquitted him. He left the court a free man and a local hero. Even the king, it is said, was impressed when he heard of the case. His luck eventually was to run out, however, and he was eventually executed at York on 4 May 1684. It is reputed that he never used violence towards his victims and was a charming man of gentlemanly appearance and bearing.

FRYSTON HALL

Sadly, Fryston Hall no longer exists as it was demolished in 1934 and its stone was used to build the Holy Cross Church in Airedale. But in the 19th century the hall had been the meeting place of the literary luminaries of the day, including such names as Lord Alfred Tennyson, Thomas Carlyle and Disraeli. Fryston Hall was the home of Richard Monckton-Milnes, 1st Baron Houghton, a poet and politician. Born in 1809, he was the son of Robert Pemberton Milnes and the Hon. Henrietta Monckton, daughter of the fourth Lord Galway.

After a private education he entered Trinity College, Cambridge, in 1827. Once he obtained his degree, he travelled abroad, spending some time at the University of Bonn. He then travelled on to Italy and Greece, publishing a volume of his experiences in the latter country in 1834 entitled *Memorials of a Tour in some parts of Greece*. On returning to London in 1837, he was elected to Parliament as member for Pontefract. He was an extremely active Member of Parliament and was particularly interested in the conditions of reformatory schools and the question of copyright. He left the Conservative party over the Corn Law issue and was from then on to align himself with Palmerston, who made him a peer in 1863.

Although a writer of some note himself, perhaps his greatest talents lay in his ability to recognise the worth of others and foster their gifts. It was through Richard that the British public were to become acquainted with the works of Ralph Waldo Emerson. He was truly a patron of literature in the traditional sense. The library at Fryston Hall was famous in its day, but the collection suffered badly in a fire in 1876. Many of the surviving books were eventually dispersed on his death, but Richard's unsurpassed collection of erotic books was kept intact and now resides in the British Library. It is said that he had owned a bookmark made from human skin and that he collected

Allison's stone ground flour mill.

autographs of executioners. He was famous for his breakfasts, which he gave at the hall, often after spending a night entertaining his male friends among the books of his library. A favourite dish served at the breakfast table was mutton pie, which as well as mutton would also contain oysters.

For seven years Richard continued a courtship with Florence Nightingale. Although she was to describe him as 'the man I adore' she refused to marry him, and so in 1851 he married the Hon. Annabel Crewe.

CASTLEFORD

The town of Castleford was founded on the site of a Roman army fort, which was named Lagentium; funeral urns dating from that period have been discovered. It is from this fort and its position, lying at the confluence of the rivers Aire and Calder, that the place gets its name – 'Castle' and 'ford'. During the English Civil War, Oliver Cromwell is thought to have placed his cannons on Redhill Plateau in Castleford to bombard Pontefract castle.

There are references to Castleford having two flour mills as far back as the 12th century. Its association with flour has continued through to the present, and even today Allinson's flour mill can be found located on the banks of the river at Castleford. This mill is the largest stone ground flour mill in the world and,

originally called Queen's Mill, it was located there in 1822 by Thomas Heptinstall. It consisted of five pairs of mill stones driven by a 20ft waterwheel and at its peak was producing 1.5 tonnes of flour an hour. The mill was taken over by the Natural Food Company in 1921: the company had been formed in 1892 by Dr Thomas Allinson (1858–1918) who believed that a diet influenced a person's health and advocated eating wholemeal bread, which although we take for granted today, was at the time considered a revolutionary idea.

Castleford is also the birthplace of the sculptor, Henry Spencer Moore. He was born on 30 July 1898 to Raymond Spencer Moore and Mary Baker. His father was a miner who was an intelligent man, being well read and determined that none of his children (there were eight in total) should work down the pit. Henry was only 11 when he decided that he was going to be a sculptor, being inspired by the work of Michelangelo. He was to become famous for his large-scale abstracts that were either cast in bronze or carved from marble. He died on 31 August 1986 at the age of 88.

THE FEATHERSTONE MASSACRE

The people of Featherstone had been collecting surface coal from the surrounding moors since mediaeval times and before. In the 1800s Featherstone developed into a mining town when deep mine shafts were sunk. By the end of the 19th century there were two mines at Featherstone: Featherstone Main owned by John

Castleford Bridge, designed by Bernard Hartley in 1805.

Shaw and Ackton Hall owned by Lord Masham. The economy of the town relied heavily on the mining industry and between the two pits employed around 1,000 men. The pits had enjoyed success and Ackton Hall was expanding; however, a downturn in the price of coal had caused the mine owners to take stock and implement drastic measures. Therefore in July 1893 the owners decided to stockpile the coal and lock out the miners in an effort to cut costs. Without welfare benefits the men were unable to support their families, and it was not long before desperation began to set in.

Time passed and the situation appeared not to be improving. Each day the disgruntled workers and their womenfolk began to congregate at the pit gates. Slowly reports were reaching the inhabitants of Featherstone from a number of other collieries in Yorkshire of violence between the miners and the owners. It was on 7 September 1893 that rumours rapidly circulated about the fact that coal was being transported from Ackton Hall to Lord Masham's mill in Bradford. This was the last straw for the 'locked-out' men, and they confronted those who were loading the wagons with coal. During this confrontation some of the wagons were overturned, and those loading them fled. Mr Holiday, the pit manager, sought help from the police in Pontefract, who were unable to help because all their available officers had already been sent to Doncaster to cover the St Leger race meeting. He was left with no alternative but to contact the police force at Wakefield. It was while there that he met Lord St Oswald, from Nostell Priory, who was also trying to get police protection for his pit. The lord suggested to Deputy Chief Constable Gill that troops should be deployed.

By the time Mr Holiday had returned to Featherstone the crowd had dispersed leaving minimal damage, a few overturned wagons and a number of broken windows. Later in the day the troops finally arrived: 3 officers and 26 men from the 1st Battalion of the South Staffordshire Regiment. Ironically, when the pits had first closed a number of men had gone to Staffordshire to work in the mines there. Crowds of locals began to gather and, keen to know what was happening, they questioned the pit manager. It appears that the mood seemed to be worsening, a situation that was not improved by the arrival of 'flying-pickets' intent on trouble. While Mr Holiday was being questioned, the troops remained quietly in the background, as they were keen not to inflame an already volatile situation. Both Mr Holiday and Sergeant Sparrow, the town's policeman, did their utmost to calm the situation as the crowd demanded that the troops left immediately. They threatened that if they did not leave voluntarily they would make them leave by force.

For a short while it appeared that the crowds had got their own way, and it seemed that the troops were leaving. It was not long, however, before it was apparent that this was not the case and they returned, marching up to the pit. The troops took refuge in the Engine House, which immediately became a target for the crowd's wrath, and the building was pelted with all manner of missiles. The crowd even set fire to a pile of timber, resulting in an urgent call to the Pontefract fire brigade to extinguish the flames. The crowd was beginning to grow, and soon the numbers had swelled to several thousand as people from neighbouring towns, hearing that something was happening in Featherstone, began to arrive. As the mood of the crowd was becoming blacker and the atmosphere growing increasingly tense, the decision was eventually taken to call the local magistrate, Bernard Hartley J.P. After failing to get the crowds to disperse, he read the Riot Act. This was a significant move as once the Riot Act had been read the crowds would have only one hour to disperse or face serious consequences, which could include life imprisonment. It appears that Mr Hartley, impatient to resolve this, did not wish to wait until the prescribed hour and promptly ordered the troops to fire a volley of warning shots.

This had no effect whatsoever on the gathered crowd, who simply jeered, believing that the troops were firing blanks. This was not, however, the case. The troops were armed with the latest bolt-action Lee-Metford rifles, the forerunner of the famous Lee-Enfield rifle that was to become the longest-serving rifle in the British Army, from 1895 to 1957. Using live ammunition, the troops opened fire on the crowds. Eight people were injured and two men, James Gibbs (22) and James Duggan (25), died from their wounds. It appears that neither of the dead men had been involved in the trouble, but had simply arrived as spectators. As James Duggan was to die in a Wakefield hospital, his inquest was carried out in the city. The verdict at the inquest was one of 'justifiable homicide'. On the other hand James Gibbs's inquest took place at Featherstone, where understandably emotions ran high. The jury was unable to return a similar verdict and pointed an accusing finger at Mr Holiday, stating that it was his over-reaction to the events that were to cause the death of an innocent man.

The backlash over the events of the Featherstone Massacre was felt as far as Parliament, and H.H. Asquith, the Home Secretary, was forced to set up a Parliamentary Commission. Unfortunately, much of the evidence given to the commission was conflicting, as each side told differing stories. As the commission was led by several friends of Asquith, it appeared that it was a 'whitewash', and it was inevitable that the miners' story would not be believed. Following the report being delivered there ensued a Commons debate. A Commons motion was called to pay compensation to the two bereaved families. Begrudgingly, the government paid out £100 to them, but Asquith made it quite clear that in no way did the compensation mean that the government admitted culpability. None of the other injured were to receive any compensation whatsoever. Asquith fared badly through this incident and acquired the nicknames, 'Assassin' Asquith and 'The Featherstone Murderer'. Some even believed that he had personally ordered the troops to open fire.

The events at Featherstone caused the Liberal Party to lose much of the working-class support and as a consequence the newly formed Labour Party began to emerge as a major political force. A few months after this unfortunate event Featherstone was visited by James Keir Hardie, who was one of the founders of the Labour party, to give a speech to a large gathering.

The lock out was to continue until November when the unions and mine owners managed to agree to a compromise. Both Alfred Holiday, the pit manager and Bernard Hartley, the magistrate, were to lose much of the respect that they had previously enjoyed. Hartley was soon to pack up and leave Pontefract for good. It was only Sergeant Sparrow who was to emerge with any respect, as he had done his level best to diffuse the situation. When he eventually retired in 1899 the local community presented him with an illuminated manuscript that recorded his role in 'the trying times of 1893'.

STANLEY FERRY

The Stanley Ferry aqueduct, built between 1836 and 1839, is reputed to be the largest aqueduct made out of cast iron. It is thought to be the first iron suspension bridge in the world. Designed by George Leather, an engineer from Bradford, and built by H. McIntosh, this impressive structure carries the Aire and Calder Navigation across the River Calder. The canal runs through a cast-iron trough, which is suspended from cast-iron arches. With a span of 165ft, a width of 24ft and the depth of 8.5ft, this structure is truly a marvellous sight. Although still in use today, a new concrete aqueduct was built in 1981, which runs by the side of the older structure. While building the new aqueduct the old one was restored.

Stanley Ferry.

During excavations in August 1838, while building the aqueduct, a mediaeval logboat (a dug-out canoe) was unearthed. Carbon dating of this oak logboat puts it around the year 990. The boat is the earliest example of a logboat fitted with ribs that has been discovered in Britain. There is also evidence that she was fitted with stabilisers, making her an ideal craft to ferry passengers across the River Calder. Considering the name of the location, it is perhaps not too far-fetched to suppose that that was her true purpose.

ALTOFTS

A short journey along a towpath from Stanley Ferry brings you to Altofts. As well as being the birthplace of Sir Martin Frobisher, pirate and adventurer, it was also the scene of the Altofts Colliery explosion of 1886. It was 3 o'clock on Saturday afternoon, 2 October, the day shift had finished, and if that had not been the case the death toll would have certainly been greater. Had it happened an hour earlier, there would have been anything up to 400 men down in the mine. As it was, there were 28 souls underground, of which 22 perished. Twenty were to die in the explosion, and two later succumbed to their injuries. It appears that it took 10 weeks for all the bodies to be removed from the mine. Recovery was painfully slow as the rescuers were hampered by the fear that there may have been fires smouldering that, once exposed to the air, would be fanned into flames, thus causing further explosions.

The verdict of the inquest was that the explosion was caused by an accumulation of coal dust in the air, which had ignited. Strangely, when the coal face was eventually examined it showed no sign of any explosion; it looked as though the workmen may have only just left after a normal day's work. In 1908 intensive tests began on the dangers of coal dust. It had always been known that coal dust was flammable, but it had never been recognised that it could also cause explosions. These tests cost £13,000 and proved conclusively that coal dust alone could cause an explosion such as that which had occurred at Altoft on that dreadful day.

THE TEXTILE INDUSTRY IN WEST YORKSHIRE

Opposite:
Finished cloth.

In truth very little is known about the origins of the textile industry in West Yorkshire. A number of primitive tools have been unearthed, which were no doubt used in the manufacture of cloth and suggest that a textile industry of sorts has been practised for many millenniums, stretching back into our distant prehistoric past. We do, however, have concrete evidence that the industry goes back at least 1,000 years, for in the porch of the parish church at Halifax there stands a stone coffin lid that dates back to 1150, on which is engraved a Celtic cross and a pair of shears, thus giving a clue to the trade of its occupant. Other evidence that supports our claims to a thriving woollen trade can be found in the written court rolls of the Manor of Wakefield. The 13th-century Calverley charters record that the village was a centre for the fulling of cloth. Ideally situated as it was, on the banks of the River Aire, there were no less than five fullers mentioned in the charters. It has been said, however, that the textile industry did not exist in West Yorkshire until the 14th century, when Edward III invited Flemish weavers to the country to encourage the production of cloth. Although there is no denying that these weavers produced a finer cloth than the coarse cloth that was commonly being manufactured indigenously at the time,

Engraving of a pair of shears on the lid of a coffin at the parish church in Halifax.

there can be no doubt that cloth manufacturing was already well established by that time.

During the 14th century, West Yorkshire enjoyed a rapid and continued expansion in the woollen trade. By the end of the next century West Yorkshire was the third-largest producer of woollen cloth in England. In 1337 restrictions were placed on the export of raw wool to continent. This was to ensure that there was a sufficient supply for local woollen manufacturers. These restrictions were to result in a reduction of the king's revenue as each sack of wool leaving the country had been heavily taxed. As a consequence the home market had to be taxed to compensate for the shortfall, and a tax of four pence was levied on each piece of cloth made and sold. To guarantee that this was properly administered the post of ulnager was

Typical West Yorkshire moorland, which is unsuitable for anything other than sheep farming.

Sculpture of a ram at Oakwell Hall.

created; this official collected the taxes due in return for a commission of a half-penny per piece. Each piece of cloth was measured and if found to be of the correct size an official seal was attached to it. The standard size of broad cloth was laid down in 1354 as being 26 to 28yds by about 4ft 10.5ins. However, it was later discovered that cloth being produced in West Yorkshire was one quarter the size of the standard piece – this smaller size was called 'Kersey' and avoided taxation. In 1393 it was decided to rectify this loophole, and 'Kersey' also became taxable with a duty of one penny levied on it. It was through the ulnagers' returns submitted during the late 14th and 15th centuries that we are able to deduce the increase of cloth production in West Yorkshire.

An understandable result of the increased trade was a general scramble for land to graze sheep. It was said that, 'The foot of sheep turns sand into gold'. Land for grazing became extremely valuable, and many villeins and freemen were to lose their 'grazing rights' to the lord of the manor. During the 18th century in this region independent clothiers living on the edge of the moors simply extended their land by taking over the otherwise useless areas of land. This was called 'in taking'; many old maps of this region label these pieces of land as 'Intak'. It is interesting to note that there are 16 Intake Lanes in West Yorkshire, which no doubt are a reference to this 18th-century practice.

In the 16th century an Act of Parliament was passed that had established that only

A wuzzy stone – a rod would be placed in a hole in the stone and a basket attached. This would be filled with wet yarn and spun to remove the excess water.

'woolstaplers' would be able to deal with wool in its raw state; however, due to much resistance by the people of West Yorkshire, there was a modification to this Halifax Act of 1555, which enabled the wool drivers to continue the practice of travelling through the region to purchase small quantities of wool, which they would sell to recognised clothiers at the market in Halifax. The clothiers would have the wool cleaned, oiled, and carded, either by their own hands or by cottagers. The prepared wool would then be despatched to homesteads throughout the region to be spun into yarn. The yarn was collected and redistributed among the home weavers to be made into cloth.

An essential process of producing woollen cloth was called 'fulling', which was to clean and thicken the cloth. This was the final step in the production of cloth and prepared it for market. The process involved two stages, which were scouring and thickening of the cloth. The scouring was to rid the cloth of dirt and oil. Originally urine was used for this stage as it was a source of ammonium salts needed to cleanse the cloth; however, by mediaeval times it was common practice to use Fuller's earth, which is

a clay-like material high in magnesium oxide and was mined in areas of greensand, more commonly found in Southern England. The next stage was the thickening, where the fibres of the wool were matted. Water was used at this stage to remove the foul smelling liquid which had been used in cleansing the cloth. The cloth would be beaten originally by the fuller's feet, hands or a club. Later this process would take place in mills where hammers, which were powered by water, were used to pound the cloth. Finally the cloth would be stretched onto frames, so as to prevent the cloth from shrinking as it dried. These frames were called 'tenters' and the cloth was attached by 'tenterhooks' – it is from this that we get our saying 'to be on tenterhooks'. Originally the 'tenters' would be left out in fields – today there are still many fields throughout West Yorkshire that are called 'Tenterfield'. According to Daniel Defoe in his book *A Tour Through the Whole Island of Great Britain*, as he approached Halifax he noted that almost every house possessed a tenter with a piece of cloth attached. It is interesting to note that in 1724 Defoe wrote, 'Be

A weaver at work.

their country hot or cold, the English woollen manufacturer clothes them all'. By 1400 many of the streams throughout West Yorkshire would have at least one fulling mill located on their banks. The early mills would have probably been dual purpose, and as well as

A handloom at the Haworth Weaving Shed.

finishing the cloth they would also undertake corn milling as well. Over time, however, mills were built for the sole purpose of fulling.

Before the arrival of the powerloom all cloth weaving would have been done by hand. If we were to travel back to a typical cloth-producing village at the beginning of the 19th century, it would still have been common to hear the rapid tapping of the flying shuttles of the handloom weavers. Although the advent of the Industrial Age was to bring many rapid changes, weaving at this time was still to some great degree a cottage industry. The last handloom weaver in West Yorkshire was said to be a gentleman named Timmy Feather, known as 'Owd Timmy', who was born on 20 January 1825. He was a tiny man (reputedly measuring less than 5ft in height) but a great character. For 70 years, until his death on 30 November 1910, he worked on his loom in his bedroom at his ivy-covered house at Stanbury above Haworth.

Weaving was a semi-skilled job and considered to be the work of the men, whereas it was usual for the women to spin the yarn. To produce the cloth, weft yarn is weaved between parallel strands of warp yarn. The word weft is derived from the Anglo-Saxon word 'Wefan' meaning 'to weave'. The weft would be thoroughly soaked prior to use, and this was to ensure that it left the bobbins smoothly and was not impeded by loose fibres. The weaver kept a bowl of water, into which he would place his bobbins. Holding them under the water with his left hand, he would hold a wooden tube called a 'bobbin sahker' (bobbin sucker) in his right. Placing the tube to his mouth, he would hold the other end to the weft. By sucking the air from the weft he ensured that it was completely soaked. This simple process did, however, require some skill as it was easy to get it badly wrong and end up with a mouthful of dirty water, which more often than not contained some very disagreeable ingredients. It is perhaps hard to believe that when a new device called the bobbin sinker was

invented, which did away with the odious task of sucking the tube, many protested against it. Traditions die hard, and progress is often feared.

Working from home it was common for a weaver to produce about five yards of cloth a day. A typical weaver's cottage would be a three-storey building in which the third floor would contain the handlooms. A common feature of the weaver's cottage would be a row of small mullioned windows on the top floor to allow good light for the weaving. Many examples of these weavers' cottages can still be seen throughout West Yorkshire. The life of the weaver was not necessarily an objectionable business. With good warp and weft, plenty of constant work and good prices, a good living could be made. Unlike the outdoor labourers their work was under shelter. Weavers enjoyed a good deal of freedom, were not tied to the clock and were able to work the hours that suited them.

As with all occupations, there could be drawbacks, trials and tribulations to be endured, especially with the introduction of the

Spinning wheel and bobbins.

Far left: Old rusty loom.

One of the displays at Haworth weaving shed.

powerlooms and mass production, which would eventually change their way of life forever. Despite determined resistance to this new progress (it is claimed that the Luddites destroyed more than 1,000 machines in one week in one mill town), the days of the handloom weavers were well and truly numbered. In Shipley a power-loom for weaving worsted was dragged through the streets before being destroyed. The cry was 'England is ruined; one man will do the work of 10, and get very little more for it.' The number of different jobs involved with the production of textiles is quite amazing, and some of the job titles were quaint and very colourful, for example: back washer, beamer, bleacher, bowl minder, burler and mender, carder, dexter, doubler, fear-nothing maker (he made rough cloth to stuff into the port holes of wooden ships), horse hair curler, horse hair weaver, knocker up, quiller (put yarns on spools), reeler, rover, riddler, scribbler, self acting minder, shearman, sizer, slubber doffer, stenterer (cloth finisher), stripper (removed rubbish from carding machines), teaser (raised the nap), twister, tozer (teaser), warper, warp dresser (repaired damaged warps) and loom tuners to name but a few. So it appears, like all progress, rather than reduce the number of workers it actually increases the numbers needed.

Although at the time many were to bemoan the loss of the hand-loom, the introduction of the power-loom was to bring new working practices that in the long run would prove a benefit to the weavers. Traditionally the weaver had been responsible for the purchase and maintenance of the looms and all the costs that this would entail. It was also expected that he would undertake all the odd jobs for no extra pay. With the introduction of the power-loom, however, the expense of purchasing and maintaining the new looms became the responsibility of the manufacturers. The expense was such that the manufacturers were reluctant to have the looms standing idle while a weaver performed some other menial task; therefore he employed others to do the odd jobs.

Finished garment on tailor's dummy.

Another important process in producing the finished cloth was that of burling. The job of the burler, which was usually undertaken by women and girls, was to remove the bits of vegetable matter and specks of dirt that became entangled in the cloth. To do this they used small irons, which had fine points, with which they could pluck out the specks. Although many of the manufacturers had burling sheds, many of the burlers were to work from home.

Although not invented here, in West Yorkshire by the mid-19th century a company owned by Edward Akroyd in Halifax was to become the worsted centre of the world. Worsted is named after a place in Norfolk called Worstead. By using longer fibres that had been combed straight and were more tightly packed, the cloth was usable straight from the loom, and unlike woollen cloth it did not need any finishing stages such as 'fulling'. This fine material was initially used mainly for ladies' garments, while the coarser woollen cloths were used for men's clothes. Later men's suits would also be made out of worsted. An attachment to the loom called a Jacquard would weave the words '100% fine worsted made in Yorkshire' along the edge of the cloth. Many tailors would ensure that that this would show on the inside edge of trouser pockets so that his customer could proudly show of the fact that his suit had been made of worsted. The finished worsted cloth had a metal 'seal' attached by a piece of string, which proved extremely popular with customers in the Far East because when the bolts of cloth were moved the seals would jangle against each other and it was thought to signify 'good luck'. Eventually the metal seals were replaced with plastic ones, which were frowned upon, and manufacturers were forced to continue using the original seals for their Oriental market. Many West Yorkshire industrialists were to make their fortunes from worsted, and to this day some of the finest worsted cloths in the world are still produced in this region.

It is said that Benjamin Law came up with the idea for shoddy while in London trying to sell flock to a saddler. While in the workshop he had noticed some of the workmen stuffing the saddles with a combination of torn-up carpets and rags, and with a sudden 'eureka' moment a great idea was born. There is some debate as to which year this took place, some putting it as early as 1809 and others as late as 1820; however, the general consensus appears to be around 1813. Whatever the true date may have been, Benjamin's idea for shoddy was to bring great wealth to his home town of Batley. The new process consisted of shredding old rags and mixing with wool to manufacture cheap cloth. This cheap cloth was destined for carpets, blankets and other heavy woollen clothes. Much of it was sent to America to fulfil the large demands for blankets in the southern slave states.

The idea of shoddy was not to be an overnight success, for many thought it was a crime to mix virgin wool with rags. It was not long, however, before opposition was to be

Once a mill producing shoddy and mungo goods.

silenced, especially when it was realised what profits could be made from this new material. By 1880 there were close to 50 mills alone producing shoddy. Regardless of the great wealth that was to be made from shoddy, it was always seen as something inferior, and its name soon became synonymous were something of poor quality and became a derogatory term that is still in use today.

It is not known for certain where 'mungo' got its name, but there is one interesting story that, although cannot be verified, is at least worth retelling. In 1860 a book was written by Samuel Jubb with the following passage: 'one of the dealers in the newly discovered material was pushing the sale of a small quantity when doubts were expressed as to its likelihood to sell, to which the possessor replied with emphasis "It mun go" meaning it must go.' There appears to be a number of variations to this tale, however, so perhaps it should be taken with a pinch of salt.

The discovery of mungo was probably in the 1830s (reputed to be the discovery of a nephew of Bernard Law, the inventor of shoddy) at which point the production of shoddy was well established. Unlike shoddy, which used dirty and worn woollen rags, mungo was able to take advantage of worsted materials and the clippings of the clothing manufacturers and tailors. These rags were unused, therefore cleaner to handle and also produced a superior material.

One of the displays in Haworth Weaving Shed.

*Goit Stock
Waterfall.*

It is commonly thought that West Yorkshire did not have a cotton industry, and it is generally said that cotton was produced in Lancashire and woollen goods in West Yorkshire. This is not strictly true, and West Yorkshire in fact did possess a healthy cotton industry. Although traditionally it had been woollen goods that had been produced east of the Pennines by the end of the 18th century, there was a growing trend towards the production of cotton, and mills that specialised in calico goods were beginning to spring up, for example, Lord Holmes Mill (or more commonly known as Gibson Mill) at Hardcastle Crags. Before long most of the towns and villages of West Yorkshire had at least one cotton mill contributing to the wealth of the region, as local entrepreneurs, aware of the growing demand for cotton goods, were not about to let good opportunities for profit slip through their fingers. There were well over 100 mills that were known to be producing cotton, although the true figure may never be known as there is a lack of detailed records. Another attraction was that there had been a growing demand for cotton warps to be used in mixed fabrics by the worsted manufacturers.

As with the development of the mills manufacturing worsted cloth, an adequate water supply was necessary to power the looms. It was therefore essential to position the mills close to a suitable water source, such as on the slope of hill to take advantage of the fast-flowing water, or near a waterfall would have been an ideal location. Goit Stock Mills in Bingley is a prime example as it is near Goit Stock Waterfall.

Sadly, the heyday of the textile industry in West Yorkshire is well and truly over. Many of the famous firms that brought so much employment to the area have long gone. Their names are but a memory of the distant past, and their mills that once were deafening with thundering machinery are now all silent: many demolished and those that are still standing have been converted into apartments, museum, galleries and wine-bars. As the mills closed, many other businesses that had sprung up to cater for the textile industry found times difficult and were forced into bankruptcy. Over 1,000 years of tradition has now gone, but the names that made this region so rich and famous live on. Names like Titus Salt, Samuel Cunliffe Lister and Edward Akroyd, giants of the Industrial Age, and men before them such as John Harrison of Leeds, left a rich legacy that we will always remember with pride.

CALDERDALE

THE RIVER CALDER

Flowing through the Calder Valley, the River Calder begins its journey on the eastern slopes of the Pennines just west of Todmorden. The river meanders through the harsh and uninhabitable moorland of West Yorkshire, interspersed as it progresses down the valley with the industrial towns and villages that once used its waters to drive the mills. After travelling some 54 miles, it eventually joins the River Aire near Castleford. It is thought that the name 'Calder' is derived from Old British (Celtic) and means 'rocky and rapid flowing water', or possibly from the Anglo-Saxon word for cold, which was 'Cald'. The two main tributaries that flow into the river along its way are the River Hebble and the River Colne. Its waters were instrumental in the success of the textile industry of the area because they provided a means of transporting materials and also, crucially, a source of power to run the mills. As such, its importance should not be underestimated. On 1 April 1974 the Metropolitan District of Calderdale was formed, taking its name from the river that had been so fundamental to the development of the area.

HALIFAX

The name Halifax does not appear in the *Domesday Book,* which might give credence to a belief that the settlement has more modern origins. There is, however, evidence that it was established in more ancient times, and scholars now agree that it was referred to in the *Domesday Book* as Feslei and was one of the nine subordinate manors or berewicks in the Wakefield Manor. The Wakefield Manor was a vast territory that incorporated a great part of the parish of Halifax, which in itself was a large area covering some 124 square miles. The parish of Halifax was one of the largest in the country and interestingly had an outline that was very similar to that of the county of Yorkshire.

Halifax has been spelt in a number of ways: Hallifax, Halyfax and Haliflax. The name Halifax means 'holy face' and refers to the legend that a portion of St John the Baptist's face was held in Halifax Parish Church as a holy relic. This is highly unlikely as, if it had been true, Halifax would have been an extremely important place, attracting pilgrims from throughout the Christian world. To confuse matters more there is another legend as to how Halifax derived its name. In 1580 William Camden was collecting information for his great work *Britannia* and was told the following story. A clergyman was spurned by a young woman he loved. Unable to persuade her to accept him, he cut off her head and hung it up in a tree. According to the storyteller, this murderous act caused it to become a place of pilgrimage, and so many people visited the place that it became a town called Hali-fax or Holy Hair. This tradition does not appear in any earlier accounts and, although it has been repeated a number of times since he penned this tale, it is more probable that the town derived its name from the earlier legends of St John. The town's coat of arms still celebrates this legend by portraying the face of the saint.

HALIFAX PARISH CHURCH

Almost 1,000 years ago the church of St John the Baptist was built to serve the people of the parish of Halifax. The original Norman church would have been much smaller than the building we can see standing today. This original edifice was demolished some time prior to 1274, when Ingelard Turbard had the parish church rebuilt. He had become vicar in that year and served the community for 40 years

Halifax Parish Church.

Far right: Old Tristram with his box, standing at the entrance still collecting for the poor.

until his death in 1316. Although the original church had been completely demolished, some of the stones from the Norman church were reused, and today we can still see the chevron stones placed randomly within the walls of the building. Over time the church enjoyed an increased prosperity, which culminated in Thomas Wilkinson rebuilding the church once again in 1438 when the south wall of the church became the north wall of the present building. A number of other additions were made over time, such as the Holdsworth Chapel on the south side and the Rokeby Chapel on the north side, which were both added in the early 16th century. Halifax Parish Church is a stunning mediaeval church that simply takes one's breath away. It is an extremely large church which

narrowly missed being designated a cathedral, that honour being awarded to Wakefield instead.

When you step through the doors of Halifax Parish Church, the first person you will probably be greeted by is Old Tristram. But do not expect a word of welcome from him as he is a 17th-century wooden effigy. It is said that he was modelled on a local beggar, by the same name, who had been licensed to beg in the precincts of the church, collecting money for the poor of Halifax. This effigy had been made of him after he had died so that he could carry on with his mission of collecting for the poor.

At the west end of the nave one will find the 15th-century font, on which stands an intricately carved wooden cover. This cover would originally been painted in a bright array of colours – reds, blues, greens and gold. During the English Civil War it was kept in a private house of a certain Mr Hartley for safe keeping and hidden away for some 10 years until it was eventually returned in 1661.

Example of a chevron stone.

George I, II, III, IV and finally William IV. John Logan spent 30 years in active service as a soldier and had been married twice, which had resulted in him having 32 children. So there he takes his well earned rest – rest in peace, John!

The font and cover in Halifax parish church.

THE HALIFAX GIBBET

'From Hell, Hull and Halifax, Good Lord deliver us', so say the words of a poem by John Taylor, written in 1622. He was referring to the infamous Gibbet Law of Halifax. His poem goes on to say:

At Halifax, the Law so sharpe doth deale,
That whoso more than thirteen pence doth steale,
They have a jyn* that wondrous quicke and well
Sends Thieves all headless unto Heav'n or Hell.
*engine

In the grounds of Halifax Parish Church is an interesting gravestone; that of John Logan, who according to the inscription died on 29 December 1830 after reaching the ripe old age of 105. The inscription goes on to say that he had lived through the reign of five kings;

The Gibbet Law grew out of a custom that was established in the time of the early Norman barons. The Earl of Warren had the royalty, as it was called, granted by the king to execute

Far left: The gravestone of John Logan.

The Halifax Gibbet.

criminals who had been caught within the boundary of his manor. The law continued to exist in Halifax long after the royalty of the Warrens had become obsolete. In the 13th century the laws of Halifax would be administered from the Moot Hall, and early records show that in 1286 John de Warren had held court there. It was in that year a certain John of Dalton was to become the first known victim of the gibbet. It was not until much later in 1541, however, that formal records of the executions were to be kept.

The gibbet was an early, but perhaps rather crude type of guillotine, which the French would make infamous in centuries to come. It consisted of an axe head that was held in a wooden block. This block would be held aloft in a wooden track and held in place by a pin. The pin was attached to a rope and when the rope was pulled by a man or beast it would release the block and axe, which would fall onto the neck of the victim below. It was a harsh law, and a culprit could have lost his head for stealing goods to the value of 13 pence or more. The condemned person could save his or her neck, however, if they were quick enough to withdraw their head before the blade fell and run across the parish boundary over the Hebble brook. As long as they were never to return to Halifax they were free. On the 29 January 1623, John Lacy achieved this seemingly impossible feat and escaped from the gibbet. Unfortunately, he was to return seven years later under the misapprehension that he had been permanently pardoned, when he had crossed the Hebble. This mistake was to cost him dearly, as without further delay he was dispatched on the Halifax gibbet. There is a public house in Halifax called 'The Running Man', which commemorates his short reprieve.

The gibbet was last used in 1650, and from when records were first kept until the final execution a total of 52 people had been despatched by this method. Today, a gibbet can still be seen in Halifax, but this is only a replica, and fortunately the blade is firmly fixed in place so that no one can lose their head. There is an interesting story connected to the Halifax gibbet concerning The Earl of Morton. He had been so impressed by this mode of execution that he had a copy made in Edinburgh to deal with the lawbreakers that were infesting the city; however, by an ironic twist of fate he was to become the first and last victim of his gibbet when he was found guilty of treason.

SHIBDEN HALL

A common feature of the larger farmer-clothier houses throughout West Yorkshire is that they were built to the mediaeval H-plan. This would consist of a central hall with an open space to the roof and a cross wing at each side; one wing being used as the service area, while the other was the family living quarters. A number of these properties were of timber-framed construction, such as that of Shibden Hall, but

A gargoyle on the side of Halifax parish is thought to represent a bagpiper. It is said that a piper would play while the condemned faced the gibbet.

decide in her favour. She had married Robert Savile, the second son of the Saviles of Elland Old Hall. So in 1504 the hall became the property of the Saviles, who were already a powerful family in West Yorkshire. Robert Savile had the walls and ceiling of the hall lined with oak and painted the ceiling sky-blue, the beams were coloured dark brown with crimson linings to the edges and the bosses were painted silver.

The house was not to remain in the hands of the Saviles for long, as their marriage produced no sons, and so the old hall was left to their daughter, Sybil. She had married into the Waterhouse family, which resulted in the hall passing into their ownership. They had made their fortune as tax-collectors and had become so wealthy that their son John was able to buy the manor of Halifax-cum-Heptonstall in 1545. He became lord of the manor for the princely sum of £150 5s 10d. The hall was to remain in the hands of the Waterhouse family until 1615 when Edward Waterhouse lost the estate through a combination of neglect and rising debts, which resulted in him being finally declared bankrupt in 1614. Eventually the estate became the property of the Lister family and remained so until 1923 when it was purchased from John Lister, who was suffering from serious financial problems. Mr A.S. McCrea, a Halifax councillor, came to the rescue of his friend John and bought the 90 acres of parkland, which he presented to the people of Halifax. He graciously allowed John and his wife to stay at the hall, and after they had both died the hall was handed to Halifax Corporation. After much debate, it was opened as a public museum on 4 June 1934.

from the 15th century onwards it became the practice to build these homes out of locally quarried stone. Many of the older timber-framed houses would simply either be encased in stone or have stone extensions added to them sometime during the 17th century.

Shibden Hall was originally built in around 1420, and it has been the home of many generations, each leaving their mark on this lovely building. It is certainly not a place frozen in time, but one that has grown and has been adapted over the centuries. Even with these changes and additions the original layout of the hall is still clear to see. It was built originally by William Otes, who had been cloth merchant, and was to remain in the family hands until the end of the 15th century, at which time there was a legal wrangle over a contested will. William's great-grandson had thought that, as a matter of course, he should have inherited the property as he was the eldest son, but a will had been left in favour of his elder half-sister from a previous marriage, and eventually the courts were to

DR JOHN FAVOUR AND HEATH GRAMMAR SCHOOL

In 1593 Dr John Favour became vicar of Halifax Parish Church, a post he held for 30 years. He was also a medical doctor and lawyer, known for his controversial views against the Roman

This is the gravestone of Thomas Bradley, the architect who designed the Square Chapel and is credited with designing the Piece Hall.

Catholic Church. Perhaps his greatest and most enduring legacy is that of being the founder of Heath Grammar School. He obtained the charter for the school from Queen Elizabeth I in 1585, bought at his own expense. The correct name of the school was originally The Free Grammar School of Queen Elizabeth; however, in 1985 the school merged to become Crossley Heath School.

THE SQUARE CHAPEL AND THE SQUARE CHURCH

Designed by Thomas Bradley when he was just 18 years old, the Square Chapel opened its doors for worship in 1772. Although the building was to have its detractors, who had thought that it cost far too much to construct, others considered it to be a resounding success. John Wesley, for one, was greatly impressed and described it as having the 'utmost elegance'. This chapel was the first building in Halifax to be built of red brick, and when first built it would have been an imposing structure, standing at

This is the gravestone of Thomas Bradley, the architect who designed the Square Chapel and is credited with designing the Piece Hall.

60ft square. At the time it could lay claim to having the longest unsupported roof span in the country.

The first pastor at the chapel was Titus Knight, who was born in 1719. From the age of seven he worked at Shibden pit and remained a collier for the next 20 years. He was a truly remarkable man, who, not letting his humble beginnings handicap him, taught himself Hebrew, Greek, Latin and classical history.

Over time the congregation outgrew the chapel, which necessitated the building of larger premises, and in 1856 a new church was built on adjacent land. It was designed by Joseph James and funded by the Crossley brothers. On 12 June 1857 the very last service was held at the Square Chapel, as the Square Church was ready to accommodate the congregation. The old building was no longer to be used as a chapel and, after having its pulpit and galleries removed, it became a Sunday school. Sadly, over the years the building suffered greatly from vandalism, arson and, having been commandeered by the army in 1939, it was left in a sorry state. For a time the fate of this historic Grade II listed building remained very much in doubt as the council, who had owned the chapel for a number of years, tried

The Square Chapel was the first red brick building in Halifax.

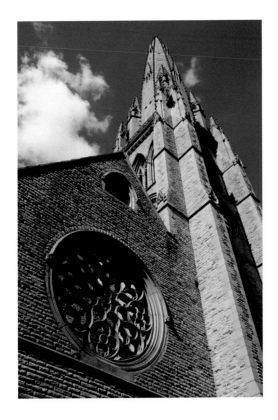

unsuccessfully on a number of occasions to gain permission to demolish it. Fortunately, its future looks rosier now, as it was bought in 1989 by the Square Chapel Trust for the paltry sum of £25 from the council, and the building has now been turned into an Arts Centre.

THE PIECE HALL

One of the most impressive buildings in Halifax is the Piece Hall. This Georgian masterpiece is thought to have been designed by Thomas Bradley, a local builder and architect. Architecturally, it is deemed one of the most outstanding 18th-century buildings in Europe. It was opened on 1 January 1779, having taken about four years to build. The merchants and manufacturers of shalloons, other worsted and woollen cloths paid for its construction at a cost of almost £12,000. The building is like an enormous amphitheatre that covers 9,144 square metres. The land had been given on lease by a Mrs Caygill, the lease being for 5,000 years at a rent of 5 shillings (25p) per annum. The

Piece Hall contained 315 rooms, and any manufacturer who paid a subscription of £28 4s 0d (£28.20) became the owner of a room. The east side of the building has three storeys, while the other sides have only two. When first opened there would have been much activity on market day, with the individual manufacturers standing in the doorways of their separate rooms waiting for potential buyers to come in and look at their stock. The smaller cloth makers had a area down below where they were able to sell two or three pieces of cloth.

Saturday was market day, and at 8 o'clock the Piece Hall doors were opened for the manufacturers to open up their rooms and arrange their stock. The small makers were charged a penny for each piece of cloth they brought to the hall. At 10 o'clock selling began with the sounding of a bell, and at noon the bell was rung again to announce the closing of the market. The cloth that had been sold could be removed up until 4 o'clock when the gates would be closed and the place left deserted until

mAll that remains of the Square Church is this impressive spire.

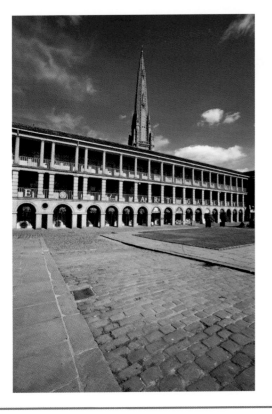

The magnificent Piece Hall at Halifax, which still draws the crowds today.

the following Saturday. There can be no doubt as to the importance of Halifax as a centre for the textile trade during the 18th and early 19th centuries. Throughout Yorkshire many milestones would state the distance to the town, for the clothiers would travel great distances to buy and sell at the Piece Hall.

As the 19th century progressed trade began to fall into decline as merchants were able to buy in large quantities directly from the mills. The sale of cotton as well as wool was permitted from 1815 in an attempt to boost sales and in 1836 the market was moved from Saturday to Wednesday. These attempts, however, proved fruitless and by 1854, although some rooms were still occupied, very little trading took place. From time to time it was used as a venue for special events, for example in 1838 when it was used to celebrate Queen Victoria's Coronation.

By 1871 it was officially renamed the Market Hall (though many still referred to it as the Piece Hall). It then became a wholesale fish, game, fruit and vegetable market and continued to be so until 1973 when the market was moved to other premises. Today, although the building has long ceased to be used for the cloth trade, it is one of the last remaining examples of a cloth hall in West Yorkshire.

SECRET MEETING AT ST CRISPIN'S INN

In 1812 a secret meeting took place at St Crispin's Inn chaired by John Baines, who was a hatter by trade. The introduction of machinery left many out of work, as each machine was able to do the work of several men. Starving and desperate, some of the men formed secret societies and were intent on bringing change to their worsening conditions. They were determined to succeed at any length and through any deed, fair or foul. They were the Luddites, and they were prepared to commit murder to further their ends.

At the meeting a Luddite from Nottingham addressed the gathered men. He told them that in his part of the country they had collected many weapons, and preparation was under way for an uprising in May. Some of the Nottingham men were planning to murder the owners of the new mills. A certain George Mellor, who had been listening to the address and was inspired by the words, proclaimed that they too should do the same. He suggested that their chosen victims should be Cartwright of Rawfold's Mill and William Horsfall, the owner of Ottiwells Mill. It was decided that they would attack Cartwright first, and on the night of Saturday 11 April 1812 they attacked Rawfold's Mill. It was a disaster from the outset for the Luddites as Cartwright was prepared for them and he had about half a dozen soldiers and a similar number of trusted workmen barricaded in the mill. The Luddites laid siege to the mill and kept up a fight until their ammunition had run out, but the alarm was raised to call the cavalry billeted close by. Without ammunition they knew that they would be no match for the cavalry. They fled, leaving the wounded behind, and it was a case of every man for himself. This was the first defeat that the Luddites had suffered, and two of their men died from their wounds.

Later in the month William Horsfall was ambushed and shot on his way home from Huddersfield market. He later died from his wounds. He had once stated the he would 'ride up to his saddle girth in Luddites' blood'. Over the coming months the armed raids continued, and the area was put under martial law. The authorities, in an effort to stamp out the Luddite terrorism, brought in an extra 1,000 troops. In October of that year the ringleaders, as well as a number of others, were arrested for the murder of William Horsfall and taken to York. The trial of the ringleaders and 63 other Luddites took place in January 1813. Out of the 66 that stood trial only seven were acquitted, 14 facing deportation, including John Baines who had presided over the meeting at St Crispin's Inn. The three ringleaders and a number of others were sent to the gallows.

CHARTISM AND THE PLUG RIOTS

There had been general disappointment among the working people when they did not receive the vote in the 1832 Reform Act. This turned to anger with the passing of the 1834 Poor Law, which established the workhouse. It faced fierce opposition from workers, religious leaders and some politicians. This unrest led to the establishment of the Chartist movement in 1836. The aim of this movement was to achieve parliamentary reforms. It was a cry for help from the working man who was bewildered by an unjust and cruel society. They were resentful of a society that had promised so much yet had delivered so little; the working man needed a cause and a belief that through Parliament changes could be made. In 1838 William Lovett drafted what was called the *People's Charter*, and their demands were:

1. Votes for all men.
2. Equal electoral districts.
3. The abolishment of the requirement that all Members of Parliament must be property owners.
4. Payment for Members of Parliament.
5. Annual general elections.
6. Secret ballots.

In the following year a petition with one and a quarter million signatures was presented with the charter to Parliament. When put to the vote it was rejected by 235 votes to 46. A general strike was threatened. In 1842 another petition, this time with over three million signatures, was submitted to Parliament, and this was also rejected. Desperation and anger had then reached such levels that it was thought that an uprising was inevitable. On 12 August 1842 a band of men and women about 20,000 strong marched on Todmorden. The following day a

Detail of North Bridge and cobbled road.

similar number marched into Halifax. They converged on the mills, stopping production by emptying the mill dams and removing the plugs from the mill boilers, thus becoming known from then on as the Plug Riots.

Troops were brought in to regain order. A group of demonstrators who had gathered on Skircoat Moor were dispersed by the troops, and 18 arrests were made. Another group of protesters were dispersed on North Bridge, Halifax, when they were faced with gunfire and a sabre charge. For the next few days Halifax remained under alert, but gradually the rioters drifted off home. A number of days later they held a large meeting at the Basin Stone on the

North Bridge and Dean Clough.

*Plaque on base
of Akroyd's
statue.*

moors above Todmorden. Although there had been some moments when it appeared that violence would break out, the feared revolution never materialised. There was a third and final attempt at submitting a petition, but this also failed and spelt the end for the movement.

EDWARD AKROYD

Edward Akroyd was born in 1810 into a wealthy textile manufacturing family. He was truly a man of his times, and like a select group of his peers, such as Sir Titus Salt and the Crossley Brothers of Dean Clough, Halifax, he was a 'philanthropic industrialist'. Edward was well read and considered by his contemporaries to be a man of taste and culture. He was greatly concerned about the conditions of the working classes and was determined to do something to improve their lot. He funded many projects, for example a school for the children of labourers, a worker's pension scheme and the first working men's college outside of London. He also created two model villages: one in Copley,

Plaque on base of Akroyd's statue.

which is situated two miles south-west of Halifax, complete with school, canteen, library and allotments, and the other at Haley Hill, Halifax, which he was to call 'Akroydon'. His model village at Copley predated the famous Saltaire project by four years, as Akroyd started its construction in 1847.

It is safe to say that he was a man of energy and drive because, apart from his good works, he had a range of interests, which included that of being a magistrate, a Member of Parliament and the Lieutenant Colonel Commandant of the local 4th West Yorkshire Volunteers. Edward was also a member of various committees, such as the Ecclesiological Society, on which he served until 1868. He also became a Fellow of the Society of Antiquaries. He could, on occasions, be prompted to acts of great pride and ego, as can be seen by his building of the stunningly ornate church of All Souls at Haley Hill. It is said that, when his main rivals the Crossley Brothers of Dean Clough (also important textile manufacturers) had erected the extravagantly lavish new Square Congregational Church in 1857 with its 235ft spire, it had driven Edward Akroyd to build something grander, employing one of the most

Statue of Edward Akroyd standing by All Souls Church, the stunning church that he was to finance completely from his own pocket.

Yorkshire Penny Bank in Bradford (now a bar).

famous architects of the day, Sir George Gilbert Scott. All Souls was eventually consecrated on 2 November 1859 at a total cost estimated to be around £100,000, which Edward had funded himself. As a final piece of one-upmanship, the spire on All Souls was 236ft high, a whole 1ft taller than his rivals' church. On top of his other achievements Akroyd also founded the Yorkshire Penny Bank (now known as the Yorkshire Bank). It had been created so as to provide a means for the working classes to save.

It must be remembered, however, that Edward Akroyd was first and foremost a manufacturer and mill-owner, and at its peak the family business of James Akroyd & Son Ltd was the largest worsted manufacturers in the world. The company had been founded in Halifax by his grandfather, James Akroyd, in 1811. This successful business had seen growth, even during the depression years of 1815–1820 following the wars with France. In 1825 James Akroyd began to supply Mr Mackintosh of Manchester with a light camlet worsted material that was to be used in the production of raincoats that became the famous 'Mac' or 'Macintoshes'. This lucrative trade was said to have netted James £34,000 in 1834. James

Akroyd died in 1836, and the business was continued by his son, Jonathan (Edward's father). Edward inherited the business with his brother Henry in 1847 when his father died suddenly at a meeting while being harassed by Chartists. When his brother retired in 1853 Edward became the sole owner of the business.

Edward married in 1838 and had Bankfield House built. Over the following years he lavished money and time on creating a magnificent mansion in the Italianate style, with elaborate ceilings, staircases and plasterwork. He built large stables in the extensive grounds and employed many servants to run his home and look after his horses. However, his fortunes changed dramatically when some of his overseas investments failed, resulting in him suffering great financial loss. His misfortune did not end there as, on falling from his horse, he received severe head injuries. With his failing health exacerbated by this fall he retired to St Leonards, in Sussex, to spend a more secluded life; where he was attended by just one manservant. It was here that he died in 1887. Edward had been a well-loved man who had spent much of his life trying to improve the

This is an ornate detail over one of the upper-floor windows that can be found on the front of a building in Boothtown, Halifax. This was where Akroyd was to locate his village 'Ackroydon'.

lives of his workers, and his funeral was attended by 15,000 people. As a sign of respect many local businesses closed for a few hours. He left an estate worth only £1,234 1s 10d but a legacy that was priceless.

DEAN CLOUGH

One of the most impressive mill complexes in Halifax is Dean Clough, which was built 1840–60. It had been built for Crossley carpets who, by 1860, were Halifax's biggest employers. The complex covered 18 acres and employed 5,000 people at the height of its success.

Born in 1772, John Crossley, the founder of Crossley Carpets, had originally been an apprentice carpet weaver for John Webster, his uncle, before taking up a position at Luddenden Foot; however, around 1800 he became manager of a carpet works in the Lower George Yard, Halifax. Four years later, the owner died very suddenly. John went into partnership with two others to keep the business going, but soon afterwards he took on a small mill at Dean

The Dean Clough Mills.

Clough with two different partners: his brother Thomas and James Travis. They traded there for about 20 years until the partnership was dissolved, and at that time the mill became his sole property. Around this time John Crossley took his three sons, John, Joseph and Francis into partnership. Machine looms were just being introduced, and the younger Crossleys were keen to take advantage of this new technology. The power loom had been an important leap forward as it reduced the cost of making carpets and therefore meant more people were able to afford one. Sadly, John Crossley senior died in 1837 before seeing his company become famous. In 1864 his sons, taking advantage of the Limited Liability Company legislation that had been passed only two years previously, formed John Crossley & Sons into a joint stock company. They were one of the first firms in the country to do so.

By 1860, Dean Clough had become a town within a town, with shops, transport and other amenities provided for its workers. Crossley's continued to use Dean Clough into the early 1980s. From then on it was destined to become a derelict site, until it was eventually bought by Sir Ernest Hall and the late Jonathan Silver in 1983. Today, Dean Clough is once more a thriving community, with its galleries, shops and theatre. It is also a business centre with the benefit of a hotel and a gymnasium. Although now completely transformed from its former days, walking around this impressive complex, with a little imagination, it is not hard to envisage those glory days when Halifax was the hub of the Crossley empire and carpets from Dean Clough found their way even into royal palaces.

THE PEOPLE'S PARK

Nowadays it is easy to forget the importance of the public park in former times, and sadly many of these have fallen into disrepair through vandalism and neglect; however, in the 19th century the public park was an oasis in the soot-

Detail of one of the water features in the park.

filled towns and cities; a restful place where the working folk could take refuge from the rigours of their working day.

There is perhaps no finer example of a public park than the People's Park. It had been the brainchild of Sir Francis Crossley who, after returning from a trip in North America, had it constructed in 1857. He had been deeply moved by the sight of the vast open spaces and stunning scenery, the likes of which he had never seen before, and had wished that he could bring the many thousands of people from Halifax to witness it. Realising this would be impossible, he decided to make a place available to them; where they might enjoy tranquil and pleasant scenery. Sir Francis employed Sir Joseph Paxton, the designer of Crystal Palace, to create the park for him. He lavished the new park with fine architecture and marble statues, and he was the first person to place such expensive works of art in a public park. At an estimated cost of around £40,000, it took a little over 12 months to construct.

The opening of the park on 14 August 1857 was treated as a great occasion, and there was a general holiday throughout Halifax. After his

Halifax's coat of arms on the building that once was a public baths next to the park.

*Detail of
fountain and
one of the many
statues in the
background.*

opening speech, Sir Francis publicly signed over the park to the Halifax Town Council for the people of Halifax to use freely forever. Over the years the park had gradually fallen into state of disrepair. Fortunately, in recent years a programme of restoration has been undertaken, and today the park is once again a place of tranquillity and magnificent surroundings.

HALIFAX TOWN HALL

In 1848 Halifax became a municipal borough, and for a number of years council meetings were held in rooms above the Woolshops. It was thought that this was not a very suitable arrangement and that it would be far better to have a purpose-built property from which to conduct the official business of the borough. At that time John Crossley (of Crossley Carpets) was the mayor, and he was the instigator of the project. So in 1863 the town hall was built. The services of Sir Charles Barry were employed to design the building, which was one of the last

buildings that he was to design, and it was to be truly a masterpiece. This exquisite building was constructed in the Italianate style and its outstanding stone carving was carried out by John Thomas. They had worked together previously on what was Sir Charles Barry's magnum opus – the Houses of Parliament.

The building was finally opened by the Prince of Wales, the future King Edward VII. The building was to have its critics; some said that it cost too much as it had cost just over £60,000, and others criticised its location, saying that the narrow streets meant that its good proportions were entirely lost. Perhaps one of the best views of this magnificent building is looking along the precinct, but even up close its elegance is evident.

OGDEN WATER

Ogden Water is well known to the people of Halifax as a local beauty spot and once was known as 'Little Switzerland' due to the pleasant backdrop of hills and woodland. It is a popular place to walk, either around the reservoir itself or along the many delightful woodland paths. While the reservoir is 34.5 acres, it is surrounded by woodlands and open moor totalling 174 acres. With just over three miles of surfaced path and track, it makes it an ideal location for walking or observing nature and provides a variety of habitats for wildlife. Ogden Waters is the home to over 130 different species of birds alone.

Work first started on the reservoir in 1854 by the Halifax Corporation as an answer to the town's dire problem of obtaining a clean source of water. Prior to that, the streets of Halifax had been nothing less than open sewers and, as with many of its neighbours, the health of the inhabitants had been a serious problem. It took four years to complete the reservoir and required a workforce of 500 men. It uses gravity to supply Halifax with its water needs as it is situated 300 metres above sea level. Capable of

Halifax Town Hall.

supplying one million gallons of drinking water, Ogden Water when full holds a staggering 222 million gallons of water.

WAINHOUSE TOWER

Perhaps one of the most well-known landmarks of Halifax is Wainhouse Tower, sometimes called Wainhouse's Folly. There is a story that it was built as a memorial for his dead wife, but the reason for the tower was more prosaic. John Edward Wainhouse had inherited the Washer Lane dye works from an uncle in 1854. Halifax Corporation was concerned at the amount of smoke in the atmosphere and was trying to bring in measures to reduce the pollution. The dye works were greatly contributing to the problem, and Wainhouse decided that it would be a good idea to build a tall chimney that would direct the smoke high up into the atmosphere and away from the populace below, and furthermore Wainhouse was determined that his tower would also be a object of beauty.

Wainhouse Tower.

In 1871 work commenced on the chimney, and to undertake the project he had employed the services of an architect called Isaac Booth. Following an argument with Wainhouse, Isaac Booth left the project and another architect called Richard Dugdale took his place. Using local stone, the tower was completed on 9 September 1875. It had cost £15,000 to build and was destined never to be used for the original purpose for which it had been designed. In 1883 John Edward Wainhouse died, and over the next few years ownership of the tower passed through a number of hands. Eventually, on 9 May 1919 ownership passed to the council, who still own it to this day. During World War Two the tower was used as an observation post. It is possible to walk up to the top and take in the magnificent views from the balcony, but be prepared for a considerable climb, as there are 403 steps to ascend.

THE ALBERT PROMENADE

Before the advent of the motor car it was fashionable for folk to take a stroll up and down the promenade or to wander through Copley Woods below. The Albert Promenade was opened in 1861 and was designed to give the people of Halifax an impressive vista of the Calder Valley. There are especially spectacular views towards Norland and Sowerby Bridge. It is still a pleasant place, though not as much frequented now as it must have been in its heyday.

ELLAND

Deriving its name from Old English, meaning 'land beside a river', the town of Elland nestles in the Calder valley. Once the centre of woollen production, in the 11th century Elland was considered even more important than its neighbours, Halifax and Huddersfield. In the 13th century Edward II granted a charter that gave Elland the right to hold a weekly market and two fairs a year. Traders wishing to sell their goods on the street would have to pay the lord's steward a fee to do so. Until the 14th century the manor of Elland belonged to the Elland family. A deadly feud between the Elland family and the Beaumonts of Huddersfield had resulted in the murders of the Ellands.

Elland was also home of the Gannex raincoat, made famous by the late Harold Wilson. The Gannex fabric was the invention of Joseph Kagan (Juozapas Kaganas), a Lithuanian Jew, who had first come to Britain to study at Leeds University in 1934. Returning to Lithuania, he had become trapped there at the outbreak of World War Two. After the war he made his way back to England with his wife, Margaret. First settling in Huddersfield, he began work as a blanket weaver. It was not long before he was opening a business at a small factory opposite Elland Town Hall; however, it was his invention of the Gannex material in 1951 that was to see his business expand and enable him to move to a larger mill on Dewsbury Road.

In 1956 Harold Wilson wore a Gannex raincoat on a world tour, and overnight it became something of a fashion icon. It was worn by world leaders such as Khrushchev, Lyndon Johnson and members of our royal family (including the corgis). Kagan soon became a multi-millionaire, was knighted in 1970 and was made a life peer six years later. Baron Kagan of Elland was later to lose his knighthood after being convicted of embezzlement and false accounting. His peerage, however, could not be forfeited, and after being released from prison he returned to the House of Lords and spoke on prison reform. He was eventually to die peacefully in his London apartment in 1995.

DOBSON'S OF ELLAND

Possibly one of the oldest remaining family-run businesses in West Yorkshire, Dobson's have been producing confectionery since 1850. It was in that year that the founder, Joseph Dobson,

The famous Yorkshire Mixtures.

accompanied by Eleanor his young bride, travelled from York to Elland. He had come to collect his inheritance, but the acting solicitor had disappeared along with his money. Without capital and at the tender age of 21, Joseph and his wife started a confectionery business. Mainly catering for Victorian family occasions, producing wedding cakes and funeral biscuits, the business began to flourish.

Neither of them were strangers to the confectionery trade. Joseph, raised by his grandparents after being orphaned at the age of 10, had worked for the confectionery firm of Craven's in York, while Eleanor came from the Berry family, who were the joint founders of Terry's. Her brother, William Charles Berry, was a confectioner and Freeman of the City of York.

Dobson's had always strived to be innovative in introducing new favours and sweet designs. For example, their 'Conversation Lozenges' had phrases on them that captured Victorian values such as 'Take ye not to strong drink' and 'Honour your parents'. In 1885, Joseph died at the age of 56. His three sons, Robert Henry, William Charles and Thomas John, all took it in turns to manage the family business. Since that time the business has been passed from father to son, a tradition that carries on to this day.

CLAY HOUSE

Clay House in Greetland, near Halifax, was built in 1650 by John Clay. It is known, however, that the Clay family lived at the site from considerably earlier times, as one Robert Clay is recorded as living there in 1216. Inside the house there can be found a plaque mentioning a Robert Clay, who was vicar of Halifax Parish Church 1624–28. On the wall of one of the rooms is a marvellous tableau that pays tribute to those who fell in World War One.

In 1597 a Romano-British altar stone was discovered near-by. It was inscribed with the following inscription:

D VICT BRIG ET NVM AVG T AVR AVRELIANVS D D PRO SE ET SVIS S MAG S • ANTONINO III ET GETA II COS

'To the goddess *Victoria Brigantia* and the divine spirit of the emperor, Titus Aurelius Aurelianus dedicated this offering for himself and his family, while Master of Sacrifices the consuls Antoninus for the third time and Geta for the second time.'

The altar stone is inscribed with the year 208. In keeping with the Roman practice of adopting local deities, it appears that the goddess referred to in the inscription is of Celtic origin, and she appears under a number of names: Brigandu, Bride, Brighid & Brigit to name but a few. The stone is now kept at Trinity College, Cambridge; a replica of this altar stone can be found near to Clay House.

RASTRICK AND BRIGHOUSE

We have plenty of evidence to suggest that there was a settlement at Rastrick as far back as Roman times and even earlier. Around 1820 Stephen Rushforth, while digging in his garden at Castle Hill, unearthed a large sepulchral urn containing a quantity of human bones. Described as 'dark-coloured', this urn measured about 14in in diameter and 20in in height. For a time he kept his find on a window sill. It appears that Mrs Rushforth was not too happy about his trophy and, whether out of superstition or reverential dread, it was soon to be safely back in the ground. Twenty three years earlier, about 20 of these urns, all containing burnt human remains, had been unearthed in the district. At the time of their discovery it was generally accepted that they would be of Roman origin. Today they are considered to be older and are undoubtedly classed as prehistoric burials.

The remains of a Roman fort have been discovered at Castle Hill, but it is uncertain whether it is the site of an earlier fortification. We do know that the Saxons made use of the earlier Roman earthworks for their defences. In the 18th century a hoard of Roman coins was discovered at Hove Edge. It appears that during the early Middle Ages Rastrick was the principal settlement, as there is no documentary evidence of the existence of Brighouse until 1240. Brighouse, once no more than a hamlet, is now the second-largest town in the metropolitan borough of Calderdale. The town name suggests a building or house next to a bridge

Clay House.

over the River Calder. Before this bridge had been built, the river had been crossed by means of a ford, called Snake Hill Ford. It is thought that this ford had formed part of the Roman route between Wakefield and Manchester. Records show that a wooden structure called Rastrick Bridge existed by 1275. This bridge was replaced by another timber bridge in 1514, with wood donated by John Hanson. In 1558 his son funded a stone bridge.

It was in 1757 that Brighouse was to receive a boost to its fortunes with the construction of the Calder and Hebble Navigation, engineered by John Smeaton. The river was providing power for the flour and textile mills, and the Calder and Hebble Navigation offered improved transportation of goods. In 1823 the Halifax and Huddersfield Turnpike Act was passed, which enabled the building of the Calder bridge. Tolls on this bridge were to be abolished 50 years later. Since its construction the bridge has been widened twice, and stones commemorating these facts can be found on it.

Brighouse possesses a number of interesting buildings, which include two churches both displaying stained glass windows from the famous William Morris factory, and designed by Dante Gabriel Rossetti, Ford Maddox Brown and Edward Burne-Jones. Many of the old mills are being converted either for retail or residential use.

BARKISLAND HALL
Built in 1638 by John Gledhill, Barkisland Hall is a stunning tribute to the wealth and prosperity of the 17th century enjoyed by the cloth merchants. Above the doorway is a Latin inscription: 'Once his, now mine, but I know not whose afterwards.' It was a Thomas Gledhill of Barkisland who married Anne Harrison, daughter of the famous Leeds benefactor John Harrison. Their son Richard Gledhill took up the Royalist cause and was killed at the Battle of Marston Moor on 2 July

1644, being knighted for gallantry just an hour before. Thomas Gledhill left much of his wealth to charity on his death in 1646. The hall has had a number of owners, including Baron Kagan of Elland, the inventor of Gannex raincoats. He bought the property in 1967 to entertain visitors and business associates.

HEPTONSTALL
High above Hebden Bridge lies the village of Heptonstall. The people of Heptonstall, like those of neighbouring villages, once derived much of their income from the textile industry as a walk through the cobbled streets will soon attest. The steep climb from the valley below is well worth the effort, as Hepstonstall is certainly a jewel with a chequered past and some dark secrets.

Walk up the street past the Cross Inn and on your left you will find the Cloth Hall. This building was originally known as the 'Blackwell Hall' after the great cloth exchange in London. Built between 1545 and 1558 by the lords of the manor it is the oldest town cloth hall in Yorkshire. Take a left turn at the cloth hall and you will come to the Grammar School. The School, now a museum, was founded in 1642 by an endowment by the Revd Charles Greenwood. When the school

An interesting carving above one of the doors at the Cross Inn.

This building was originally the cloth hall.

Far right: Pinnacle that was brought down by lightning.

Originally the grammar school, now a museum.

finally closed in 1889 the building then became a branch of the Yorkshire Penny Bank. It was eventually given to the council in 1954.

Heptonstall is one of the few places in the country where there are two churches in the same grounds. The first church, which now lies in ruins, was built in the 13th century and dedicated to St Thomas a Becket who had been murdered in 1170. Significant rebuilding of the church took place in the 14th and 15th centuries (for example, the tower had been heightened to accommodate bells, which had been paid for by a local man, William del Bryge). During the English Civil War the church had been covered with sheepskins to protect it against the Royalists' cannonballs. Following the Restoration, when Parliament agreed to restore the monarchy, there had been a growth in small groups of people gathering together to worship in their own way. With that there was a increase in the Nonconformists which meant that, although the church was tolerated, it was no longer much loved and fell into disrepair. So much so that by the time John

Wesley preached here it appears that he was not that overly impressed as he remarked that 'it is the ugliest church I know'. By the 19th century the church had deteriorated so much that it lost its roof in a great storm in 1847.

It is said that over 100,000 bodies were buried in the churchyard of St Thomas a Becket's. Perhaps none so infamous as that of 'King' David Hartley, the leader of the notorious Halifax coiners, although the actual whereabouts of his grave is a closely guarded secret. It is said locally that, from a cottage next to the churchyard the coiners carried out their nefarious deeds; of coffins leaving the premises at the dead of night, fully laden only to return empty. Taking old gold coins, the coiners would take clippings from their edges and melt them down to make new ones. It was this crime that eventually led to the introduction of milled edges to coins, which would make any defacement immediately apparent.

The new church took four years to complete at a cost of £6,000 and was consecrated by the

Bishop of Ripon, the Rt Revd Dr Longley, in 1854. It had been built in the Gothic style and dedicated to St Thomas the Apostle. In 1875 lightning struck the south-west corner of the tower and brought down a huge pinnacle, which can be seen today standing nearby.

One of Heptonstall's most famous landmarks is undoubtedly the Methodist chapel. It is the oldest Methodist chapel in continuous use in the world. The foundation stone of the chapel was laid by John Wesley himself and was built in an octagonal shape so that the devil would have no corner in which to hide. Completed in 1764, the worshippers at the chapel on their departure were presented with stunning views of the landscape below and a powerful symbol of 'God's Grace'.

CRAGG VALE

The peaceful surroundings of Cragg Vale today belie its dark and sinister past. In the mid-18th century it was home to the Halifax coiners and in particular home to their leader the notorious 'King' David Hartley and his brother Isaac, known as the 'Duke of York'. Over the centuries

there have been attempts to give the activities of the coiners an air of romanticism and derring-do, but in truth this is a sorry tale of cruel, cowardly and treacherous individuals and their crimes, which included murder and betrayal.

St John the Baptist in the wilderness – Cragg Vale.

Obviously they would not leave evidence of their dark doings about their houses, and it may well be that some old gold coins still lie hidden in some Cragg Vale wall.

Taking a guinea, they cut shavings of gold from the edge with a pair of shears. Filing a new edge to the coin, it was then returned into circulation. The gold shavings were melted and made into new coins; more often than not being made into foreign coins. During the 18th century it was common to see foreign coins such as Portuguese moidores or Spanish doubloons in circulation in England. Cragg Vale was an ideal location for the coiners as it was close enough to Halifax, where the currency could be easily obtained and returned, but isolated enough to give the miscreants protection. The government was reluctant to do anything about this practice, and it was not until an exciseman named William Dighton was murdered by the coiners that they were finally prompted into action. William Dighton had been determined to bring these criminals to justice, but when he arrested 'King David' and another coiner named Jagger on Saturday 14 October 1769 his fate was sealed. The coiners had been nervous at the actions of Dighton, but with the arrests Isaac Hartley was determined to be rid of the excise man. Two assassins were found willing to do the deed, and on 9 November Robert Thomas and Matthew Normanton laid in wait to ambush Dighton. He was close to home when he was attacked by his assailants, and it was Normanton who fired the fatal shot. Before making their escape the two men looted the dead man's pockets. It was not long before the two murderers were betrayed and taken into captivity. James Broadbent was a local man who had turned informer; a treacherous man, keen to collect the £200 reward that had been offered. Unfortunately, his evidence proved to be untrustworthy, and so the pair were subsequently acquitted. They were arrested two years later, however, when fresh

The White Lion – a traditional coaching house dating from 1657.

evidence emerged. Under English law they could not be tried again for the same crime, but they were then found guilty of highway robbery, having robbed Drighton's pockets, so they were hanged anyway.

Perhaps the most heinous of the crimes of the coiners was the sadistic murder of a labourer who had been bragging that he knew the identity of the murderers. The gang cornered him in a blacksmith's forge and held his head under the flames with heated tongs clamped around his neck. They then finished the poor soul off by filling his breeches with red hot coals. Most of the coiners were either hung, sent to prison or deported. Isaac Hartley escaped justice as there was never enough evidence to obtain his conviction, so he remained a free man for the rest of his life, dying at the age of 78 in Mytholmroyd.

HEBDEN BRIDGE

Hebden Bridge was not a settlement until the early 19th century, prior to which it had merely been a river crossing for the pack horses laden with cloth and food. The first bridge built there was made of wood, but in 1510 it was replaced by a stone bridge, which can still be seen today. This is the old 16th-century packhorse bridge that straddles Hebden Waters, which gives the town its name. The oldest and main settlement in the area was Heptonstall, high on the hill above. It was not until 1643 that Hebden Bridge was 'put on the map' when a battle between the Royalists and Parliamentarians was fought

there. Colonel Bradshaw and his Roundheads won the day. The Cavaliers fled the field of battle with the Colonel and his men in hot pursuit. Many of the Royalist army lost their lives that day, either by being trampled under foot in the rout or plunging from the narrow bridge to drown in the swollen river below.

Before the coming of the Industrial Age, Hebden Bridge's only importance was the bridge and the White Lion Hotel, a traditional coaching inn dating from 1657. Things changed with the coming of machinery, new roads and methods of transport. Prior to this, the textile industry had been restricted to home-spinning, handloom weaving and had been located high in the hills but mechanisation needed a source of power – water. This meant that locating the new mills in the base of valleys became the logical and obvious choice. With the subsequent construction of railways, canals and better roads the transporting of cloth became less problematic.

At its height there were more than 30 mills in Hebden Bridge, and the smoke from their chimneys filled the Calder Valley with thick acrid fumes. The pollution was so bad that it was said that the only time you were able to see the town from the hills was during Wakes Week, when all the mills would shut down for the traditional holiday. Because of the number of mills and the fact that Hebden Bridge was surrounded by hills, space was at a premium. This left little room for the workers' houses, and consequently they were built on the steep slopes of the hills. This led to a novel solution to the problem and the construction of 'top and bottom' or 'double-decker' houses, where one house was built on top of another. The town was renowned for the production of cotton material, namely hard-wearing fustian and corduroy. The looms now lie silent, and today the town has become the 'capital' of Upper Calderdale and famous for its bohemian lifestyle.

The 'double-decker' houses built on the steep slopes of Hebden Bridge.

GIBSON MILL AT HARDCASTLE CRAGS

Deep in the heart of Hardcastle Crags lies Gibson Mill, or to give it its correct title Lord Holme Mill. Built in 1800 by Abraham Gibson, this mill was one of the 'first generation' mills of the Industrial Revolution. The mill is located in a beautiful wooded valley amid crags of millstone grit and was driven by an internal water wheel powered by Hebden Water. Cotton

Gibson's Mill and mill pond.

cloth was produced at Gibson Mill until 1890 when it was turned into a place of entertainment for the local people. Its facilities included a dance hall, dining room, roller skating rink, refreshment kiosks and boating on the old mill pond. This was a far cry from its role at the height of the Industrial Revolution, when it employed 21 workers toiling an average of 72 hours per week.

Today the mill is owned by the National Trust and with its 'hands-on' exhibitions gives the visitor a thrilling experience of the mill's industrial past and people who worked there. An official guide from 1899 stated: 'Near the Crags a quaint little Mill is passed, called Lord Holme Mill, but better known as Gibson Mill. Some think that it spoils the beauty of the spot, others that it adds to the picturesqueness. This is a matter which we must therefore leave for the taste of the tourist himself.' Whatever your view is, there is no denying that Hardcastle Crags is a delightful place to spend some time, even if it is only to experience the walks taking

in its natural beauty. Though for the present-day visitor it is perhaps a little hard to believe that this historic mill standing in such idyllic surroundings could have once been a 'dark satanic mill' notorious for its harsh conditions.

LUDDENDEN

The village of Luddenden stands halfway between Halifax and Hebden Bridge. The name Luddenden means 'Loud Waters' and refers to the brook that it stands beside. There is no mention of the village in the *Domesday Book*, which leads us to believe that this is not an ancient village. Luddenden received its first mention in 1274, at which time it was the site of what was possibly the oldest corn mill in the parish of Halifax. It was owned by the lord of the manor of Warley, and it was compulsory that all corn that was grown on his manor was ground there. The mill was rebuilt in 1633 by Henry and Jane Murgatroyd. Houses now stand on the site of the mill, and all that remains of it is a lintel and a millstone.

Far right: Millstone and lintel at Luddenden.

The delightful Hardcastle Crags in autumn – there are a number of walks in this stunning woodland.

Oats Royd Mill.

Today it is hard to believe that this sleepy village was once a hive of activity. With the coming of the Industrial Revolution there was a rapid growth in population. The period brought great change to the locality, and many mills were built, bringing in workers from other areas. One of the largest mills was Oats Royd Mill, where the manufacturing of worsted goods took place between 1847 and 1982. Although it was partially burnt down in 1989, it is currently being converted into apartments.

Central to village life would have been the church, and for many years the people in the surrounding areas would have had to travel to Halifax to worship. In the 15th century permission was given to build a church at Luddenden, which was intended to serve the communities of Midgley and Warley. St Mary's Church has gone through many transformations during the centuries, and the building that we can see today was built at the beginning of the 19th century. This was the third building on this site and was completed in 1817. Designed by Thomas Taylor, a notable architect from Leeds, it was built in the Gothic style. Over the years the church has undergone further alterations.

Born in Luddenden on 21 June 1705, David Hartley (not to be confused with 'King' David

Rope drum from Oats Royd Mill, now standing in the centre of Luddenden as a monument.

Far right: The Rushbearing cart.

St Mary's at Luddenden.

Hartley, the Halifax coiner) was to become one of the most influential philosophers of his day. His father, also called David, was the vicar of St Mary's from 1698 to 1706. After studying at Cambridge, where he received an MA, he went on to practise medicine at Bury St Edmunds, London and Bath. In 1749 he wrote his seminal book *Observations on Man, his Frame, his Duty and his Expectations*. Joseph Priestley (1733–1803), the man credited with discovering oxygen, remarked that Hartley's book had taught him more than any other, with the exception of the Bible. The book became a 'must read' for Unitarians and took a central place in their curriculum of study. In fact, the poet Samuel Taylor Coleridge, who had converted to Unitarianism while at Cambridge, can be seen holding a copy of the *Observations* in his portrait and called his first son David Hartley Coleridge. Despite the high esteem that his contemporaries held for him, after his death in 1757, the work of David Hartley was sadly largely forgotten.

THE RUSHBEARING FESTIVAL

A tradition that had almost completely died out was the Sowerby Bridge Rushbearing Festival. Fortunately, the tradition was re-introduced in 1977, and the colourful festival can be seen each September. The Rushbearing cart, which is at the centre of the festivities, is pulled through the streets of Sowerby Bridge accompanied by music and Morris dancers. The tradition goes back to the days when the earthen or flagstone floors were covered with rushes to offer some warmth. Prior to the 15th century churches would not have pews for the worshippers to sit on and, as wooden floors would be rare, the congregation would have to kneel on the bare floors, which would be extremely uncomfortable. As only the rich could afford cushions, rushes were used as a cheap way of covering the floor. From time to time the rushes had to be replaced as they soon become unhygienic. So from this need to replace the rushes grew the celebration of Rushbearing. Today, only token rushes are presented to the churches as the procession makes its way through the local villages, stopping of course at the various hostelries along the way for regular refreshment.

TODMORDEN

Although Todmorden lies within the borders of West Yorkshire, historically things have not been so clear cut. Until the border was moved by the

Local Government Act of 1888 the boundary between Yorkshire and Lancashire actually ran through the centre of Todmorden. Even today, Todmorden has an Oldham postcode and a Rochdale telephone code (both places being in Lancashire). It was in 1641 that the name Todmorden first appeared, and prior to that it had been known as Tottemerden, Totmardene, Totmereden, Totmerden or Totmerden. There are various theories to what the name may mean; one thought is that it comes from Old English and means 'the marshy home of the fox', but the most popular theory is that it actually means 'Totta's boundary valley'. The latter is probably the closest as it would probably refer to the valley created by the River Calder, which runs through the centre of the town.

For many centuries Todmorden was a mere village surrounded by isolated farms. It was not until the early 19th century, with better transport systems and the coming of machinery, that it experienced great growth. Because of its closeness to Lancashire and particularly Manchester, where there was a ready source of materials and trade, the main output of the town was cotton. But, as we have already seen in an earlier chapter, there was a healthy cotton industry throughout West Yorkshire.

Possibly one of the most influential families in Todmorden in the early 19th century were the Fielden family. John Fielden, born in 1784, was a social reformer and benefactor. Along with his brothers, he introduced the power loom into the Calder Valley in 1829, thus creating a 'dynasty' in the cotton industry and becoming a very wealthy man. As with many of his contemporaries and industrial rivals, John Fielden was also involved with politics and he was a Member of Parliament for Oldham between 1832 and 1847. He wrote a book entitled *The Mischiefs and Iniquities of Paper Money*, which was published in 1832, and four years later he wrote a 152-page booklet called *The Curse of the Factory System*. A group was

The stunning Todmorden Town Hall.

sent by the government to investigate whether he had incited, encouraged or supported a local riot. But they were unable to find any concrete evidence to implicate him as the town folk closed ranks against these outsiders. During the cotton famine in the 1860s that had been brought on by the American Civil War the Fielden family paid unemployed workers to build roads and buildings in Todmorden.

Perhaps Todmorden's most stunning landmark is its town hall – an architectural masterpiece. Designed by John Gibson of Westminster, this impressive building straddles the River Calder. When it was built, half of the building was in Lancashire and half in Yorkshire until the boundary was moved on 1 January 1888. At the top of this fine building is a magnificent pediment with ornately carved figures. At the centre of the scene are two female figures: one representing Lancashire and the other Yorkshire. Initially it had been intended to be built as a public hall with a market hall beneath. The scheme failed due to a number of

The magnificent town hall pediment with its carved fresco.

organ in their chapel. This act was in opposition to John Wesley's own immortal words:

Still let us on our guard be found,
And watch against the power of sound,
With sacred jealousy;
Lest haply science should damp our zeal,
And music's charms bewitch and steal
Our hearts away from thee.

The new chapel at Lumbutts was such a success that by 1877 it was demolished to be replaced with a larger building, which can still be seen today. Inside the chapel stands a 3-tonne organ called *The Old Lady of Lumbutts*, which has stood there for about 100 years and is still in good working order.

LUMBUTTS MILL

Originally the site of an old corn mill, its potential was soon recognised when purchased by the Fielden Brothers in 1796. Before long they had developed a spinning mill and in 1806 had even increased the capacity of the old mill

reasons, including the American Civil War, which had caused a cotton famine. In 1866 the Fielden family purchased the partially constructed building and rebuilt it as the town hall. It was officially opened on 3 April 1875 at a final cost of £54,000.

Once, Todmorden was bristling with chimneys and mills, but now most of them have gone and the few mills that still remain no longer support a vibrant textile industry, having been put to other uses.

Far right: The waterwheel tower at Lumbutts.

Lumbutts Chapel.

A CHAPEL AT LUMBUTTS

The original chapel at Lumbutts was opened on 9 July 1837 and was the result of dissention among the Methodist community. This dissention had been sparked off in the late 1820s when Methodists at Leeds installed an

dam, therefore enabling the mill to run for longer each day. Ten years later they were to construct a larger dam upstream and at a much higher level. The mill already possessed a 40ft water wheel, which was considered the largest they could safely use, and it was Samuel Fielden who came up with idea of using two smaller wheels. Constructing a tower on the eastern side of the mill, he mounted two 30ft Fairburn water wheels. These were fitted with geared teeth, enabling one wheel to drive the other. Eventually, a third 30ft wheel was added and the height of the tower was further increased. At a height in excess of 90ft, it was one of the tallest buildings in the area.

At the end of the Industrial Age there were only two out of the original four mills still working. Both of them were owned by the Fielden Brothers and produced weft for their large weaving sheds in Todmorden. The end of World War One saw a demise in the fortunes of the Fieldens, and by 1926 the two mills at Lumbutts were closed. During World War Two the mills were used for government storage, and after the war one of the remaining mills was demolished. All that was left was the manager's house and the water wheel tower. In 1989 the services of the late Fred Dibnah, the famous and charismatic steeplejack from Bolton, were employed to survey the old water wheel tower. The intention was to repair and make safe the old building. Erecting six ladders with ropes and metal staples, Fred proceeded to examine the fabric, after which he commented that 'The fabric is in remarkably good condition, the worst damage being caused not by time, wind and weather, but mindless vandalism.' In June 1990 he proceeded to put things right and restored it once more.

THE BRIDESTONES AT TODMORDEN

Standing high above Todmorden are the Bridestones or, as known locally, the Kebs. The

The Bridestones, known locally as the 'Kebs'.

main stone (known as the Bride) is like an up-turned bottle and you can almost get your arms around the narrowest part of this 4m boulder. A smaller boulder lies by its side and is known as the room.

SOURHALL ISOLATION HOSPITAL

In 1874 a smallpox epidemic broke out in Todmorden, which left 32 people dead. In a

The oldest man-made artefact in the area – the weathered 'celtic' cross.

Stoodley Pike.

meeting chaired by the local vicar, Revd Molesworth, it was decided to raise money for the victims and their families and to make provision to isolate the cases to stop the spread of the disease. Shortly after the meeting, a grant of £700 was made by the Local Board, which was used to purchase a building. Originally it was called Peel Mill and had formerly been a factory making pickers to be used in the new power looms. It was a two-storey building, which was converted to hold 16 smallpox patients, and became known as the Sourhall Isolation Hospital.

Originally, the sole purpose of the hospital was to isolate the smallpox outbreak and to contain the disease. However, over the coming years there was a decline in smallpox so it was decided to admit patients suffering from other contagious diseases such as typhoid and later diphtheria. It remained a hospital until after World War Two, when in 1949 the hospital closed and the building was converted into private dwellings.

STOODLEY PIKE

There is one landmark in Calderdale that is hard to miss as it can be seen for literally miles. Stoodley Pike Monument is one of the tallest hillside monuments and stands at 100ft. The monument overlooks Todmorden and Erringden Moor and can easily be seen from Hebden Bridge and Heptonstall. The original monument was built by public subscription in 1814 after the defeat of Napoleon at the Battle of Leipzig; however, it fell down in 1854. The monument that we see today was designed by James Green, a local architect, in 1856 and was to celebrate the end of the Crimean War.

It is possible to walk to Stoodley Pike, and as you get close it is hard not to be impressed by this huge monument which had been built using local millstone grit. There is a doorway in one of the sides which leads to a spiral staircase. Walk up the stairs and you will emerge onto a balcony that goes around the monument. The views of Calderdale from this viewpoint are simply breathtaking. Sadly, over the years the monument has suffered damage through thoughtless people carving their names in the stone and other mindless forms of graffiti.

WILLIAM DEARDEN

Born on 15 October 1803 at Hebden Bridge, William Dearden, from an early age, showed a keen interest in the classics. Educated at Heptonstall Grammar School, he was to build a reputation as a poet, especially of the narrative verse. The *Star-Seer*, a long, five-part poem written in 1837, was much praised by his contemporaries such as William Wordsworth. It was very loosely based on local tradition, which he furnished with copious notes to explain the references in the text.

William Dearden was a close friend of the Brontë family, and it is known that he shared a common interest in the metaphysical with certain members of the family. He always maintained a belief that Branwell had played some part in co-writing *Wuthering Heights*. In 1844 he wrote *The Vale of Caldene; or, the Past and the Present,* which was a tribute to the upper Calder Valley. In this six-volume work he laments the loss of the landscape to industrial development, his boyhood home of Weasel Hall having been demolished to make way for the railway. Dearden was an early educationalist and set up a boarding school at The Hollins, Luddenden. For a time he was President of the Huddersfield Literary and Philosophical Society, and later he became Principal of Warley Grammar School, a position that he held until his death in 1889. Sadly, it appears that his work is now out of print.

KIRKLEES

Kirklees is one of the five metropolitan boroughs of West Yorkshire, with a population of nearly 400,000; it is the most populated district of England that does not have a city status. Kirklees is mainly made up of old mill towns, though there are a few rural villages such as Denby Dale. It is also the location of Kirklees Priory, which is said to be where Robin Hood was callously murdered by the evil Prioress. Folklore has it that they were cousins. It is probable, however, that it had not been her intention to kill him, but as was common medical practice of the day she simply 'bled him' – unfortunately, she bled him too much. Sadly, all that is left of the priory is the gatehouse. It is rumoured that it was in one of the upper rooms of this gatehouse that Robin passed away. Not far from it lies his grave, from which the original gravestone has long since gone. However, to the rear of the grave is an inscription which says:

'Here underneath dis laitl stean Laz robert earl of Huntintun Ne'er arcir ver as hie sa geud An pipl kauld im robin heud Sick utlawz as his as iz men Vil england nivr si agen Obiit 24 Kal. Dekembris 1247'

According to tradition, the dying Robin fired an arrow from his death bed, and where it landed he commanded was to be his grave. He had asked his loyal Little John to make sure that his dying wish was carried out. However, there is some doubt about the validity of the story as the grave lies some 600 yards from the gatehouse – a distance considered too far for a long-bow shot, especially uphill. There are some who maintain that the position of the original grave has been moved. Perhaps we will never know. Unfortunately, the gatehouse and Robin's grave are on private property and not open to the public.

Founded in the 12th century for Cistercian nuns, it is doubtful that Kirklees Priory was ever very large, as at the time of the Dissolution the community still had no more than seven nuns. Excavations carried out in the mid-20th century confirmed that the church was around 80ft long. It is thought that the living accommodation was equally modest. The gatehouse is thought to be the only part of the priory that remains, but as this is of a later design, which is either Elizabethan or Jacobean, we can conclude that it would not have been part of it. It is a large building, but as it was built in later days and possibly belonged to a house it would certainly not be indicative of the size of the priory. If this is the case then it throws some doubt on the validity of the legend of Robin firing his arrow to mark his grave from it, as it would not have been built yet.

ST PETER'S OF HARTSHEAD

This is a little gem of a church and is well worth a visit. There has been a church at this site since Saxon times, but it was the Normans who first built a stone church at this spot. Unfortunately, all that remains of the original Norman church are the south doorway and chancel arch. As the only surviving examples of Norman ecclesiastical architecture in the diocese, their importance cannot be exaggerated. It is difficult

St Peter's at Hartshead.

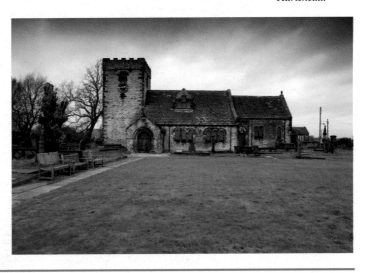

A fantastically gnarled and weathered dead tree stands in the churchyard.

to accurately date the square tower; however, it is believed that it may be mediaeval. The majority of the church was rebuilt in the 19th century in the Neo-Norman manner. Using this style they were able to take full advantage of the surviving original features. Another feature of this church that gives it its distinctive look is the 'dormer-type' window in the roof.

Located in the foothills of the Pennines, the church is open to all that the elements can throw at it. This quaint church would not be out of place in a Brontë novel, and in fact between 1810 and 1815 the vicar of St Peter's was the Revd Patrick Brontë, father of the famous Brontë sisters. The church also has another famous connection – with Robin Hood. Although it is not known whether he would have ever worshipped there, it is believed that he would have been acquainted with this delightful building, for he was not a stranger to these parts and, as we have already mentioned, is thought to be buried in close vicinity in the grounds of the Kirklees estate. Not far from the

Batley Parish Church.

church the Walton stone can be found. This intricately carved stone is all that remains of what is believed to be a Saxon preaching cross. The cross itself has long since vanished, and all that remains is the plinth that once held it. Time has faded the carvings, but a close inspection still reveals an elaborate Saxon tree carving surrounded by fine lattice-work.

BATLEY

Batley was established on the banks of the River Calder and it has had a long association with the textile trade. It was mentioned in the *Domesday Book* as 'Bateleia', with a population of just 40 people. There has been a place of worship at this site since at least the 11th century, but the church we see today was built during the reign of Henry VI. In 1612 the Revd William Lee founded Batley Grammar School, originally as a boys' school. The school became co-educational in 1996. It has taught a number of famous pupils, perhaps the most notable of them being Joseph Priestley, the discoverer of oxygen.

In the 1740s Batley was introduced to Methodism, and it was not long before it had taken a strong hold of the town. In fact, so strong was its influence that even today there are areas of the town that are still noted for the absence of public houses. Since early times, the main occupations of the town had been weaving and farming. The late 18th century brought great changes to Batley with the coming of the Industrial Age. In 1796 it saw the arrival of the first water-powered mills. It was, however,

during the 19th century that the town would experience its greatest prosperity, when it became a centre for the 'shoddy' trade. The inventor of the 'shoddy' process, Benjamin Law, was born at Birstall, a close neighbour of Batley.

A town hall was built in 1853, and was constructed in the Neo-Classical style, complete with corbelled parapet, pilasters and a centre pediment. Batley once possessed a coal mining industry, the records of which go back to the 16th century. The last coal mine in the area closed in 1973.

BIRSTALL

Birstall was the birthplace of both Joseph Priestley and Benjamin Law, and has played a significant role in the history of West Yorkshire. Originally a Saxon settlement, it was possibly fortified, as its original name of 'Burg-Steall' meaning 'place of fortified homestead' certainly suggests. There can be no doubt that it was a Christian settlement, as the remains of a stone base of a Saxon preaching cross can be found in

the grounds of the present church. It has been suggested that the settlement was fortified to protect its inhabitants against the heathen king Penda.

In the early 12th century the first stone church was built. All that remains of this original building is the lower part of the tower. It is known that, in total, the church has been rebuilt four times. It was originally dedicated to St Peter and St Paul, but its dedication to St Paul was dropped during Tudor times. This church is well within walking distance of the centre of Birstall and is well worth a visit. In the porch there are a number of interesting gargoyles, and in the church grounds can be found many remarkable tombs, notably those of three Knight Hospitallers dating from the 14th century.

In the town centre there can be found a statue to one of its famous sons: Joseph Priestley. Born in 1733, he was to become theologian, natural philosopher, educator, dissenting clergyman, political theorist and scientist: a polymath of extraordinary breadth

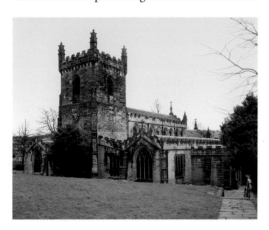

Far left: St Peter's at Birstall.

Gargoyle in the porch of St Peter's.

and scope. Throughout his career he was to publish over 150 works; he discovered oxygen and cemented his scientific reputation with the invention of soda water. It is, however, for his discovery of oxygen (or 'dephlogisticated air' as he called it) that he is perhaps most remembered. After being educated at Batley Grammar School, he joined the dissenting ministry. Over the following years he was constantly moving throughout England, and his travels even took him to Europe on a number of occasions. It was while teaching at an academy in Warrington that he first became interested in chemistry. A strong believer in free thinking and toleration, combined with the sometimes controversial nature of his publications, often brought him into conflict with the authorities and the public. In 1791 he was forced to flee to America when an angry mob had burnt down his church and home. He continued to live there until his death in 1804, at which time he was a member of every major scientific society in the world. His writings were

to influence many leading philosophers and great thinkers such as John Stuart Mill, Herbert Spencer and Immanuel Kant, to name but a few.

Benjamin Law, the inventor of 'shoddy', was born in Gomersal in the parish of Birstall. On 8 November 1773 he was baptised at Birstall Parish Church, his parents being George Law and Mary Wilby. His father was a clothier who had learnt his trade from his father. Unfortunately Benjamin was only 15 when his father died, so it is probable that from then on he was apprenticed to another clothier. It was not long after his father's death that he moved to the parish of Batley, where it is recorded that he was married at the age of 17 to Rachel Stubley. It appears that his wife had previously had a child out of wedlock, as it is recorded that a child had been baptised seven months earlier. Although it will never be known for certain, many believe the child to be his. The marriage of Benjamin and Rachel took place on 13 June 1791. Rachael was five years older than Benjamin. Sadly, Rachel was to die six

Statue of Joseph Priestley.

Far right: Memorial to Rachel Stubley, wife of Benjamin Law.

years later, at the age of 28. A memorial can be found in Batley Parish churchyard with the following inscription: '*In memory of Rachel the wife of Benjamin Law of Havercroft Who departed this life on the 22nd day of October 1797 In the 28th year of her age. Also of Sarah their daughter who died in her infancy*'.

The common practice of the day was for widowers to re-marry quite quickly, especially if they had small children to bring up. It is known that Benjamin had at least two very young children at the time of his wife's death. In 1801 he married Lydia Sheard from the parish of Leeds. They had 12 children together and so, including the children he had with his first wife, he had 17 children all told. The family left Batley around 1830, and Benjamin died in Stockport seven years later. His widow returned to Batley and died there in 1849. It is for the invention of the 'shoddy' trade that Benjamin Law will be forever remembered and, as a consequence, for his part in the prosperity of the region. Today, anything that is called 'shoddy' is regarded as something that is poorly made and of inferior quality, but to our forefathers it was something that could bring great wealth.

OAKWELL HALL

For the last 100 years or so, Oakwell Hall has been the subject of much debate between architects and historians. It was the inspiration for 'Fieldhead' in Charlotte Brontë's novel *Shirley*, where she described it as being 'neither a grand nor a comfortable house; within as without it was antique, rambling and incommodious'. According to a set of initials and a date that appear on the porch, the house was built by John Batt in 1583. Analysis of the great beams in the roof suggests that the timbers were felled in the spring of 1583, which appears to confirm the year of construction. It also dispels a once held belief that this was a timber-framed building that had been encased in stone

Oakwell Hall.

at a later date. This had been a common practice in West Yorkshire, and a number of our great stone buildings had started life in this way.

Oakwell Hall is a typical mediaeval house of the gentry, with its large central hall rising up to the roof, although records from 1611 indicate that it had once been floored across at balcony height. The hall remained the property of the Batt family until the beginning of the 18th century, when in 1707 the estate was split up. Oakwell Hall was then left to slowly decay. By the 19th century it was being used as a girls' school; this was to prove fortunate for the hall, because if it had been a private residence it would have undoubtedly been modernised in the style of the day, and we would have lost many of its outstanding features. It was while visiting a friend, who was a pupil at the school, that Charlotte Brontë first became acquainted with Oakwell Hall and its surroundings.

One legend concerning the hall is that of the ghost of William Batt, who in 1684 was the owner of the house. A young man of 25, he was away in London when on 9 December 1684 he was killed in a duel. That very evening his ghostly apparition strode along the lane, through into the hall and up to his room, where he vanished, and only a bloodstained footprint remained. Records show that he had been at the Black Swan in Holborn the day he had died and that he had borrowed some money. Oliver

The coat of arms of the Warenne family, shown on a stained-glass window at Dewsbury Minster.

Heywood, a local diarist, had written two entries concerning the death of William Batt, one saying that he had died 'in sport', and the other that he had been killed by Mr Gream at Barnet near London. William's body lies in Birstall.

The hall is in 110 acres of pleasant parkland, which is made up of woodlands, streams, pastureland, ponds and bridleways. Today it is an attraction for visitors wishing to experience the delights of this diverse environment. There are a number of walks, one of which leads to the English Civil War battlefield of Adwalton Moor.

DEWSBURY

Founded by St Paulinus on the banks of the River Calder in 627, Dewsbury was established as a Christian community. St Paulinus was a Christian missionary who had left Italy in 601 at the bidding of Pope Gregory the Great. His mission was to assist St Augustine in his work of converting the pagans. He was described as being a 'tall man with a slight stoop, who had black hair, a thin face and a narrow, aquiline

Dewsbury Minster.

nose, his presence being venerable and awe-inspiring'. It was not for a number of years, however, that he was to venture to the North. He spent many years in Kent helping St Augustine with his work. It was when the daughter of King Aethelbert of Kent married the pagan Northumbrian King Edwin that St Paulinus was required to head north as her chaplain. From there he began his conversion of the North. There are still a number of stone preaching crosses to be found in the area, but perhaps the most important is the fragment that records: '*Hic Paulinus praedicavit et celebravit*', meaning 'Here Paulinus preached and celebrated'. He died on 10 October 644.

During Saxon times Dewsbury enjoyed great status, and the Parish of Dewsbury extended over a large area covering Huddersfield, Mirfield and Bradford. On the banks of the River Calder stands Dewsbury Minster, or All Souls Church, where St Paulinus preached. The church itself dates back to the 13th century, and it has a bell called the *Devil's Knell*, which is rung each Christmas Eve. It is rung once for each year and is a tradition dating back to the 15th century. The bell was donated by Sir Thomas de Soothill, a local knight, as a penance for murdering a

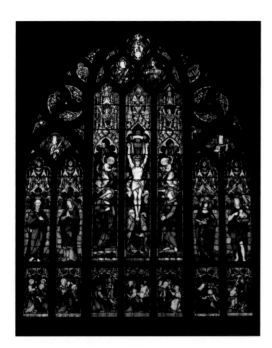

Stained-glass window – Dewsbury Minster.

servant boy by drowning him in a mill pond in a fit of rage. Originally called *Black Tom*, the tenor bell was to be rung at Sir Thomas's funeral but is now rung on Christmas Eve to celebrate the Devil's departure from earth. It takes a team of sturdy bell-ringers to accomplish the feat, for it can take a few hours to complete, and they must finish on the stroke of midnight.

A market for local clothiers was established at Dewsbury in the 14th century, but two outbreaks of the plague, one in 1593 and the other 10 years later, caused it to close. It was not reopened until 1741. Dewsbury retained a degree of ecclesiastical importance throughout the Middle Ages and collected tithes from as far away as Halifax. During the 18th century it became a Methodist stronghold, and John Wesley was to visit Dewsbury on a number of occasions, the Centenary Chapel being built to commemorate his visits.

An important development in the growth of Dewsbury was the completion of a short branch of the Calder and Hebble Navigation. The opening of this branch in 1770 meant that Dewsbury now had access to the main distribution centres of Hull and Manchester, and was well placed to take full advantage of the

coming of the Industrial Revolution. It proved not to be plain sailing for the town, as during the early 19th century it witnessed social instability and was one of the centres of the Luddite disturbances. Once more, in the 1830s, it experienced tension and agitation when it became a centre for the Chartist movement's agitators. Despite all this instability, Dewsbury still benefitted from the fruits of the Industrial Age. With its excellent transport system and the development of the 'shoddy' industry (that of taking old rags and mixing them with new wool), Dewsbury was soon to be the centre of the heavy woollen industry. There was a great demand for blankets and uniforms, and 'shoddy' was an ideal material with which to fulfil this demand. The arrival of the railway brought an improved transport system that Dewsbury was quick to adopt. Eventually the town was to have four stations, one being just for goods, but now only one remains, and that is the Wellington Road Station. In 1837 the local firm of Richard Baker and Son pioneered the use of

A sculpture by Jason Thomson entitled Flirting with the Past *– a celebration of Dewsbury history.*

fibreglass, from which they made stunning ladies' headdresses and ornaments. They presented a glass apron to Queen Victoria that was so fine it looked and felt like silk.

As with many of the Victorian buildings that were constructed throughout the main industrial towns and cities of West Yorkshire, Dewsbury has many fine examples of architecture that reflect its prosperity. Many of these grand buildings survive and we can still marvel at their splendour. Much of this stunning architecture is a tribute to the great industrialists who brought prosperity to the region. Throughout both the 19th century and a great part of the 20th century the woollen industry was still mainly run by family businesses. However, during the early 1950s the industry fell into crisis as the price of wool from Australia increased. There had been something of a revival of fortunes during the 1960s, but the 1973 oil crisis spelt the final demise of this great industry.

CHRISTOPHER SAXTON

Considered to be the father of British cartography, Christopher Saxton was born in the early 1540s at Dewsbury. He was the first person to undertake a comprehensive survey of the counties of England and Wales. Publishing his landmark atlas in 1579, his precision, artistry and attention to detail was unprecedented. This was the first atlas that was solely devoted to a complete depiction of one country. Setting the standards for all atlases to follow, this masterpiece is still regarded as a groundbreaking achievement.

Christopher grew up in Dunningley, near Dewsbury, where his association with John Rudd, the local vicar and a keen amateur cartographer, gave him an early interest in map-making. He went on to be educated at Cambridge. His abilities were soon noticed by Thomas Seckford, Royal Surveyor to the Queen, and Thomas took him under his wing. State officials were beginning to realise the importance of accurate maps for political and administrative purposes. Queen

Elizabeth I was also enthusiastic about the advantages to be gained through accurate maps, and she wanted an atlas to be produced that would reflect national prominence and pride. In 1573 Christopher was selected to produce such a monumental undertaking.

He was to achieve an unrivalled standard of accuracy, which hitherto had been thought impossible, and considering he had worked without the benefit of modern cartographic technology this was no mean feat. Each image in his atlas was endorsed with the Royal Arms, signalling that the work was of the highest standard. Each page was painstakingly drawn so as to fully convey the topographical relief. Towns were depicted by delicate clusters of red buildings and the countryside highlighted with groups of trees. He brought his seas alive with fanciful sea-creatures and ships. The work was a stunning masterpiece and is considered by many to be the benchmark of map-making even today. The whole survey took only six years to complete, which was indeed a significant achievement in itself.

CLECKHEATON AND THE SPEN VALLEY

Cleckheaton is situated in the Spen Valley, along with its neighbours Heckmondwike and Liversedge, and together they are more commonly known as 'Cleckheckmondsedge'. This was a name originally coined by J.B. Priestley and was intended to represent an archetypal West Yorkshire mill town. There was a rapid growth of industry in the area after the discovery of good quality coal was made in the north of the valley. Occupying a central position among the great manufacturing towns of West Yorkshire during the 19th century, the valley was ideally placed to share in their prosperity. As with its other neighbours throughout West Yorkshire, the area was heavily involved in the production of woollen goods. At the beginning of the 19th century the Spen Valley also became involved with the manufacture of cotton. One of the main advantages of this was that it was light, which made it an ideal material for more elderly or infirm workers to handle.

By the mid-19th century the town of Cleckheaton was reputed to be the carding centre of the world. It is thought that this trade was introduced into this area by the Overend family as far back as 1698. There were to be as many as 11 carding factories in the town by 1838. This was to be a profitable business, and one that would make the fortunes of many businessmen. The workforce, however, was mainly made up of children, who would earn a pittance, and it was only the best of these young workers who could hope to earn enough to keep themselves from starvation. The work was hard, and it was said that 'it required sixteen hundred deft movements to earn a halfpenny'. The children would place staples in the leather, which were used to card the wool, and the long monotonous days of toil would leave many of the weaker children deformed and crippled.

Many of the large and impressive buildings, which were erected at the height of the region's prosperity, are still standing today. These were to become symbols of wealth, and one striking example was Cleckheaton's Town Hall, which was to occupy a prominent position in the community. The townsfolk thought that it would be fitting to erect this fine building on the auspicious occasion of Queen Victoria's jubilee. The total cost of the hall and its furnishings was £13,900, and the money needed was raised by public subscription. This was made possible by the Town Hall Committee,

which was led by their energetic chairman Mr Elymas Wadsworth. On 21 June 1890 William Anderton JP, a leading figure in the town, laid the foundation stone. It was due to Mr Wadsworth's enthusiasm, however, that this project was at all possible, though sadly he never saw it it through to fruition as he passed away before it was completed. There could have been no doubt in the minds of the people who assembled at the opening ceremony of the finished building that if Mr Wadsworth had been alive that day the honour of leading the proceedings would have fallen to him. Later that year there was to be another gathering, when the leading figures of the town met to witness the inauguration of a clock which had been placed at the top of the building. It had been presented to the town by Wadsworth's sons as a memorial to their father.

Many people in the area were Nonconformists, such as Methodists and Baptists. The leader and founder of the Methodist Church, John Wesley, was a regular

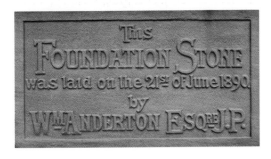

Far left: The foundation stone of Cleckheaton Town Hall.

Cleckheaton Town Hall clock tower.

*The Upper
Independent
Chapel at
Heckmondwike.*

visitor to the region. Quakerism was also widespread throughout the district and even now a few Quaker burial grounds from the 17th and 18th centuries still remain. The valley also possessed many chapels, which catered for the numerous denominations, and a number of these fine buildings are standing today, such as the Upper Independent Chapel at Heckmondwike. This stupendous structure has now been converted into apartments.

Although, as mentioned above, the region was to enjoy great prosperity during the 19th century, by the 1920s this had come to an end. By this time industry was on the decline, a number of the local pits had been closed and the textile industry was suffering badly. It was not long before the textile mills and foundries were closing. Today many of the old mills have been renovated and turned into either apartments or shopping centres.

JOHN CURWEN

Who can forget Julie Andrews singing *Doe, a deer, a female deer* from *The Sound of Music*? Well, if it had not been for a certain John Curwen we might never have had this song. Born in Heckmondwike on 14 November 1816, he was to devise the Tonic Sol-fa system as an aid to sight-reading. His father, Spedding Curwen,

*Monument to
John Curwen in
Green Park,
Heckmondwike.*

was a Nonconformist minister, a vocation that John would take up in 1838. It was through his experience with Sunday school teachers that he realised there was a need for a simplified method of teaching somebody how to sing by note. He believed that music should be available to all, regardless of age or class. The Tonic Sol-fa was based on a number of other musical systems, most notably that of Sarah Ann Glover (1785–1867), whose method John had used to teach himself how to sight-read.

In 1843 he brought out his *Grammar of Vocal Music,* and 10 years later he started the Tonic Sol-fa Association. He published the *Standard Course of Lessons on the Tonic Sol-fa Method of Teaching to Sing* in 1858, and as well as producing a number of other publications he opened a college in 1879 to teach his system. His son, John Spencer Curwen (1847–1916), was later to become principal of the college. John resigned from his post as a minister in 1864 to concentrate fully on promoting his system. In 1863 he set up the J. Curwen & Sons publishing

firm, which was to continue as the Curwen Press into the 1970s. He died on 16 May 1880 and is remembered by a memorial that can be found in Green Park, Heckmondwike.

HOLMFIRTH

Perhaps best known as the setting for the long-running TV series *Last of the Summer Wine*, Holmfirth was originally established around a 13th-century corn mill and bridge. Three centuries later there was rapid growth there as the village took advantage of the growing cloth industry and the cutting of stone from the local quarries. In the early 20th century it was well-known for its film industry, as at that time West Yorkshire was, surprisingly, the Hollywood of its day. The firm of Bamforths, based in Holmfirth, was an early pioneer of film-making, and it is thought that they were the inventors of film editing with their 1899 film called *The Kiss in the Tunnel*. Eventually they gave up making films in favour of producing cheeky seaside postcards, which proved to be a very lucrative trade for them.

Flooding has always been a problem for Holmfirth and its inhabitants. The earliest recorded flooding was in 1738, when rainstorms caused the banks of the River Holme to burst. Fortunately there was no loss of life at that time, but much farmland was damaged. Thirty-nine years later the River Holme burst its banks once more, and this time three people drowned, while the stone church that had been built in 1476 was swept away in the deluge. Tragically, in 1852 the inhabitants of the Holme Valley were to experience the worst flood of all with the loss of 81 people in the raging waters. The embankment of the Bilberry Reservoir had collapsed, releasing 86 million gallons of water that destroyed the centre of Holmfirth. Many people were left homeless and without work, for the flood had destroyed mills, shops and houses. After the disaster an inquest decided that the tragedy was the result of defective construction of the reservoir, and then went onto say that, 'the

Commissioners, in permitting the Bilberry Reservoir to remain in a dangerous state with the full knowledge thereof, and not lowering the waste pit, have been guilty of great and culpable negligence'. There was also loss of life in the flooding of 1944, when three people perished in the flash-flooding following a thunderstorm. Due to reporting restrictions in place at the time, and the fact that the Normandy invasion was to take place a week later, the flood was not widely reported. There was widespread damage to property, but it is suggested that the reservoir prevented the flood from being more serious than it was. A local teenage boy was awarded the George Cross, the highest civil recognition, for his part in the attempts to save the life of an elderly lady. Tragically both his father and the lady perished during the rescue attempt. There were a number of German POWs from a camp near Sheffield who were drafted in to help with the rescue of local inhabitants and property. For a brief time the hostilities were forgotten as the prisoners worked side by side with the locals to restore order to the town. Locals would bring steaming cups of tea to the young German captives, and cigarettes and other treats would be surreptitiously slipped into the pockets of their greatcoats.

To the south of Holmfirth there are a number of small villages, which for a time enjoyed considerable success with handloom weaving. Although this cottage industry fell into decline due to mechanisation in the 19th century, a number of good examples of weavers' cottages can still be found in places such as Honley, Scholes, Jackson Bridge and Hepworth. These dwellings are typical of the traditional design: the weaving room at the top of a two or three-storey building and rows of narrow, mullioned windows to allow maximum light into the room. Often the weaving room would be reached by outside stairs and a 'taking in' door allowed easier access for woollen yarn to be taken in and the woven cloth removed.

During the 16th and 17th centuries it was common for many of the families to make a

Far right: Huddersfield's coat of arms.

Now the Colne Valley Museum, these former weavers' cottages illustrate the rows of narrow mullioned windows.

living through both textiles and farming. The land was mostly poor and unsuitable for growing crops; therefore, the smallholders turned to dairy cows or sheep to supplement their incomes. It was common for many of the weavers to work from yarn that had been spun from the fleeces of their own sheep. Throughout the Holme Valley can be seen a number of farmsteads known as 'laithe houses'. These substantial properties would combine family living quarters, a hay barn and a weaving room – all under one roof.

HUDDERSFIELD

There is a romantic notion that Huddersfield owes its name to Uther Pendragon, the father of the legendary King Arthur. This unlikely theory is possibly derived from the fact that in a broad Yorkshire dialect Huddersfield is pronounced 'Uthersfilt'. It is, however, more likely that the origins of the name are rather prosaic. The *Domesday Book* has the name as 'Oderesfelt', and it was probably the name of the person who had owned the field. It is interesting to note that

in 1318 John del Cloughes, who at the time was lord of the manor, referred to Huddersfield as 'Hodresfield'. The earliest settlement appears to have been established around Castle Hill at Almondbury, which can be seen easily when standing in the centre of modern Huddersfield. Upon the hill there is evidence that there was a fort of Celtic origin. From between 56BC and AD43 the summit of Castle Hill was surrounded by defensive ditches and banks. Cartimandua, the Queen of the Brigantes, had her citadel within this hill fort. The fort was destroyed by fire in 74 by Venutius after he had defeated the Brigantian queen. Just to the north of Huddersfield there is evidence of a Roman settlement at Slack. The name of the settlement was Cambodunum, and it is believed that the word was derived from the name of the British war god Camul and the Celtic word for strength, 'dun'. A Roman altar was discovered there in 1736 by Revd Watson, an historian from Halifax. Other findings over the years have suggested that this may have been the location of a Roman fort. It is thought that the garrison at Slack would have contained about 500 men, but it appears that the fort was abandoned around the year 140.

After the Romans left Britain the fortunes of Huddersfield fluctuated over the coming centuries, first being in the hands of the Angles, then under Dane control; however, by the time of the *Domesday Book* Huddersfield was laid to waste. We cannot be certain what Huddersfield was like at that time as there is very scant information. We do know that the land had been given to Ilbert de Lacy by William the Conqueror for services rendered during the conquest and in subsequent struggles subduing the locals. He was also to receive a number of other manors throughout Yorkshire, including Leeds and Bradford. But the *Domesday Book* makes no mention of there being a church at Huddersfield, which would indicate its lack of importance. There were a number of small churches in surrounding settlements. It was generally accepted that Dewsbury was the ecclesiastical centre for the region and, even today, Huddersfield still pays a tribute to the mother church in Dewsbury each year. It is clear that by the latter part of the 13th century there was a church in the town, as in 1288 the Pope had ordered a survey of church property. Huddersfield Parish Church was valued at £9 6s 8d (equivalent to approximately £9.33 in modern currency). It is said the church at Huddersfield was built to fulfil a promise: Walter de Lacy had been out riding his horse when he fell into a swamp. Struggling to escape and in danger of drowning, he vowed that if he should escape he would build a church on his father's land. Extricating himself from the quagmire, he was as good as his word. It is recorded that the first vicar of Huddersfield was Michael de Wakefield in 1216.

It appears that for many centuries Almondbury would have possibly been the more important of the two settlements. From as early as 1294 Henry de Lacy had received a grant from the king to hold a weekly market at Almondbury. Little is known about the market other than it was held each Monday. As it was to

Huddersfield's market cross.

be nearly 400 years before Huddersfield would receive its own Royal Charter to hold a weekly market, it does tend to suggest that, of the two, Almondbury was the more important. After 1671 Almondbury's importance began to wane. Huddersfield's location was better suited for the market, as travelling downhill laden with goods must have been markedly easier than toiling uphill to Almondbury.

Prior to the building of the Cloth Hall in 1766, cloth appears to have been sold in the churchyard of Huddersfield Parish. It is said that traditionally clothiers were only permitted to sell their goods from the churchyard wall, but as time passed and trade increased it became common for tombstones to become commandeered as shop counters. This inevitably caused indignation and much friction with the locals. It is thought that this was one of the major factors in building the Cloth Hall, so as to stamp out this practice.

In the early 19th century Huddersfield saw some troubled times with the Luddite insurrection. This unrest culminated with foul murder in April 1812 when four of the confederates, George Mellor, William Thorpe,

The Concert Hall entrance.

Thomas Smith and Benjamin Walker (also known as Ben O'Bucks), decided attacking machinery was not enough. Their victim was a certain Mr Horsfall, a manufacturer of Marsden. They ambushed him as he was riding home and inflicted numerous gunshot wounds on him. Mr Rowland Houghton, a surgeon from Huddersfield, while trying to save Mr Horsfall's life, noted the extent of his wounds: 'two wounds to the upper part of the left thigh, another on the lower part of the belly, another on the lower part of the scrotum and two more on the right thigh.' There were also a number of other smaller wounds. Mr Horsfall died from his injuries the following day at Warren House Inn. His assailants disappeared and there appeared to be a lack of sympathy for the dead man, as even the offer of a massive £2,000 reward failed to bring forth any witnesses. It was only through the persistence of the local magistrate, Joseph Radcliffe, that the attackers were brought to justice: persistence and more than a little help from Benjamin Walker, who turned King's evidence to save his neck. The other three were hanged in January 1813. Walker did not receive his reward and spent the

rest of his life as a vagabond in rags – an outcast for evermore.

The years that followed were a time of general unrest, and at the dead of night in June 1817 several hundred cloth workers marched on Huddersfield, rallying to the cry of 'Now lads, all England is in arms, our liberties are secure, the rich will be poor, the poor will be rich.' What followed became known as the 'Folly Hall Fight', but an old account sheds a different light on it. The local yeomanry had ridden down to disperse the rebels and met them on the bridge at Folly Hall. A few pistols were discharged, and the yeomanry made a hasty retreat and, according to the words of a contemporary witness, 'galloped up Chapel Hill as if they were riding a steeplechase.' It was not long before military reinforcements were mustered and the rebels quickly disbanded. During the next few days a number of arrests were made, but all of those arrested were acquitted.

Built in the classic Italianate style, Huddersfield Town Hall was clearly built in two

A lion holding a shield outside Huddersfield Town Hall.

Above the door of the Prudential building.

Huddersfield boasts what was once the largest Wesleyan Chapel in the world. Built in 1819 by Joseph Kaye, it is now known as the Lawrence Batley Theatre complete with a bar, restaurant and exhibitions. Perhaps one of the most unusual buildings in Huddersfield is that of the Prudential Assurance as, unlike many of its contemporaries that were built in stone, this building was constructed in terracotta and red brick. It was built at the end of the 19th century by the prominent architect Alfred Waterhouse, who famously designed the Natural History Museum in London. One of the most imposing and magnificent buildings in Huddersfield is the railway station, which is truly a 'stately home for

stages. Designed by the architect John H. Abbey, the first stage of this wonderful building was constructed between 1875 and 1876; the next stage was started two years later and it was completed in 1881. Inside the town hall is a sumptuously ornate concert hall, which is home to the Huddersfield Choral Society.

Originally the county court building, the Old Court Brewhouse was built in 1825 and was constructed in typical Georgian style with small paned sash windows. Today it is possible to have a drink in the old courtroom, and many of its old features still remain.

Far left: Now the Lawrence Batley Theatre, this building was once the largest Methodist chapel in the world.

A figure on the side of the Prudential building.

Far right:
Statue of
Harold Wilson.

Huddersfield
railway station.

trains'. Built between 1846 and 1850, it is one of the finest stations to be found outside of London. The visitor to this elegant building is greeted by eight stunning Corinthian columns, an unquestionably magnificent sight. The central library was opened on 15 April 1940 by Mayor Alderman Norman Crossley, and the first book borrowed was *Take Courage* by Phyllis Bentley (considering the year perhaps a very apt choice). The author was born in Halifax in 1894 and was renowned for setting her novels in the Calder and Colne valleys. At the main entrance of the library stand two sculptures by the artist James Woodford (1893–1976), depicting art and literature.

Today Huddersfield is a busy university town with a great tradition for industry. As the late Rt

Hon Harold Wilson had said of his home town, 'a great industrial community, bound together by pride and skill.' A statue of this former prime minister stands prominently in front of Huddersfield railway station.

CASTLE HILL

As previously mentioned, Castle Hill was where the British Queen Cartimandua had had her fort and palace. However, excavation of the site in the latter part of the 1930s established that there had been a small fort at Castle Hill as far back as 200BC. Although small in size, many experts consider this Iron Age fort to be West Yorkshire's most important early hill fort. Over the centuries defences were improved and the fort expanded in size. By the time the Romans had arrived in Britain, the fort would have been an impressive affair and a fine example of the technology of its day, with double drystone walls and ditches with sharp stakes to defend against chariot attacks. It appears that the occupants of this fort may have employed the Gaulish method of firing the stone

One of James
Woodford's
statues outside
the library.

walls, which created a solid clinker core and consequently gave it greater strength. Despite being a heavily defended fort, it appears that Cartimandua submitted to the Romans without a fight.

In the year 43 the Emperor Claudius started the conquest of Britain. A number of kings immediately submitted to Roman rule and are referred to on a triumphal arch built for Claudius in Rome. It is believed that Cartimandua was one of them. According to the Roman senator and historian Tacitus, she was of 'noble birth' and had inherited her kingdom rather than come to it by marriage. Tacitus went on to describe Cartimandua and her husband Venutius as loyal to Rome. Indeed, when a certain resistance leader named Caratacus, who had been fighting the Romans in Wales, had sought sanctuary with her she immediately handed him over to the Romans. Her loyalty was rewarded with great wealth. A few years later she was to divorce her husband and replace him with his armour-bearer. She held Venutius' brother and a number of other relatives as hostages, but this did not stop Venutius from declaring war on her. It was only through the intervention of her Roman allies that she was able to retain her throne and defeat her ex-husband; however, during a period of Roman instability and the so-called 'Year of the Four Emperors', in the year 69, Venutius took full advantage of the unrest and again declared war. Cartimandua requested help from the Romans, but as a result of the instability they were only able to send auxiliaries. Unable to defeat Venutius, they evacuated the British Queen and left her ex-husband in control of the area. It was at this point that she effectively disappears from the history books.

In 1897 Queen Victoria had reigned longer than any other monarch. A number of prominent citizens of Huddersfield decided that a monument in the shape of a tower should be built to celebrate the Queen's Diamond Jubilee. The site suggested for the monument was Castle

Victoria Tower on Castle Hill.

Hill. The suggestion did not meet with unanimous approval and the lord of the manor was known to have voiced his dissent. The idea was not new as in 1849 a scheme had been conceived to construct an 80ft tower to be called the 'Victoria Prospect Tower'. The tower was to include a museum, observation terrace,

Detail of Victoria Tower.

The grave of Enoch Taylor.

refreshment rooms and private rooms for subscribers. The new tower was to be at least 100ft high. Although a private company was formed to complete the project, the scheme eventually came to nothing. There was opposition from a number of people who considered it a waste of money that would be better spent on the construction of a building such as a public library. Despite this opposition the tower was built. It was opened by the Earl of Scarborough on 24 June 1899. Sometimes referred to as the Jubilee Tower, its correct name is the Victoria Tower. This prominent feature is still, to this day, dominant on the landscape.

MARSDEN

Although there is evidence of human activity in the area of Marsden going back at least 8,000 years, as a settlement the village can only be traced back to around the mid-15th century. At that time it was a royal hunting ground, and in 1433 a chapel was built where the labourers could worship. This saved them from the long trek to Almondbury Parish Church. By the mid-16th century the population of Marsden had grown to around 400 people. The village stocks can be found outside Wessenden Court in the village centre and are thought to date from around 1557.

As with many settlements in West Yorkshire, the cloth industry played an important role in Marsden's prosperity. There are still examples

The 16th-century stocks at Marsden.

of weavers' cottages to be found in the village; their distinctive top floors with unbroken rows of windows were designed to gain maximum light for the workers. The first mill to be built in Marsden was Hey Green in 1710. Sadly, all that remains of this once magnificent building are the stables and the mill dam. A larger church was built in 1758 to accommodate a growing population. The new church had bare earth floors so that the dead could be buried inside the chapel. Soon there was no space left as the village folk preferred to inter their dead within the confines of the building. In the late 18th century Marsden was blighted with the Black Fever which killed about 300 people. Because the graveyard was too small to accommodate the dead, the level was raised by bringing in soil from around the village so that further burials could take place.

In 1760 the first coach road was made through Marsden, which travelled from Huddersfield to Manchester. The road was constructed by the famous Blind Jack of Knaresborough; this blind man was not only renowned as a musician but also as a constructor of highways. The Industrial Revolution brought great prosperity to Marsden but also brought unrest through the activities of the Luddites. This led to the murder of a local mill owner, Enoch Taylor, in 1812. Such was the hatred of Enoch Taylor that the Luddites called their machine-breaking mallets 'Enoch'. Marsden's industrialisation continued throughout most of the 20th century; however, with the decline of the textile industry in the 1960s the village's fortunes declined markedly. Recently Marsden has seen an upturn, as much of the land that had once been occupied by the great mills has been used to build private estates to accommodate commuters to the nearby cities. Also, being the location for the TV series *Where the Heart is* has given it a healthy tourist industry.

MARSDEN PACKHORSE BRIDGE

As the name suggests, packhorse bridges were built so that horses laden with goods could cross rivers. These stone bridges tended to be just wide enough for a horse to pass, with low parapets to give ample clearance to the horse's panniers. Generally these bridges were built on trade routes (also called packhorse routes) and for many centuries were the backbone of our transport system. Mellor Bridge at Marsden is an excellent example of a packhorse bridge.

MELTHAM

Although the township of Meltham was the location for a number of 18th and 19th-century mills and the home of the famous David Brown Tractor factory, it has retained something of the rural in its character. It is located below Wessenden Moor and lies about five miles south-west of Huddersfield. The area of Meltham has been inhabited since time immemorial and the town is overlooked by two Iron Age sites. In the *Domesday Book* it was referred to as Meltha, and it consisted of four carucates of land to be taxed. A carucate was the unit of measure used to assess the worth of a place. Derived from the word 'caruca', which was Latin for plough, it was the area that a plough team could cover in an agricultural year, which was notionally considered to be 120 acres. It appears, though, that it was not a precise measurement, and a carucate could vary from area to area and even sometimes even within the same manor. The *Domesday Book*

Mellor Bridge – a packhorse bridge at Marsden.

went on to say that it was waste, and also that there was a wood pasture that was two miles long and one and a half miles wide.

Meltham can boast one of the oldest brass bands in the world, as the Meltham and Meltham Mills Brass Band was founded in 1846. In 1827 the Meltham Mills Provident Co-operative Society was formed, which predated the famous Rochdale 'Pioneers' by 17 years. Perhaps Meltham is best known as the home of the David Brown Tractors, with over half a million tractors being built and shipped to more than a 100 countries. David Brown Tractors played a critical role during World War Two as it was the sole producer of some vital gearing for Spitfires. It is surprising, therefore, that they were never to be a target for the Luftwaffe. In fact, the only bombs to be dropped in the Kirklees area were when a German bomber, en route to Liverpool, was caught in the beam of an anti-aircraft spotlight and it disposed of its load in a panic. Sadly, the factory closed in 1988 and almost 50 years of tractor history came to an

A view of the tower through the trees.

A memorial to the 140 who succumbed to the plague.

The 19th-century church at Mirfield, with the old mediaeval tower standing next to it.

end. Even so, engineering is still a major industry in Meltham, as is the textile industry, although now other industries have made Meltham their home, including a motor racing team.

MIRFIELD

Mirfield was among the 214 manors given to Ilbert de Lacy by William the Conqueror for his part in the conquest and subjugation of the English people. Evidence of a motte and bailey castle that de Lacy constructed can still be seen standing beside the parish church. It is thought that he used the mound and moat of a previous fortification on which to build his new castle. Mirfield's motto is 'Fruges ecce paludis', meaning 'Behold the fruits of the marsh', and gives credence to the belief that the name Mirfield means 'clearing near a swamp or marsh'.

It was not until the late 13th century that Mirfield had its own church. Prior to that date its inhabitants would have had to travel to Dewsbury to worship. Tradition has it that the wife of Sir John de Heton was robbed while on her way to Dewsbury, which prompted Sir John to petition the Pope for a grant to build a church at Mirfield. It was to serve the community until 1826, when it was replaced, but the original mediaeval tower was kept. This new church was to be demolished a number of years later, and Sir Gilbert Scott was employed

to design another place of worship. At Sir Gilbert's insistence, the mediaeval tower was yet again saved and can still be seen today. Built in 1871, the church cost £22,000 to complete. Standing in the Lady Chapel beneath the 16th-century *Book of Homilies* is the Mirfield Stone. It is believed that the Mirfield Stone is an 11th-century grave monument. Standing 2ft 6.5in tall and carved on all four sides, this monument is of great importance as it is the only known example of its kind from this period. A slab can also be found in the Lady Chapel which commemorates those who died in the 1631 plague.

By the 14th century Mirfield was an important centre for the woollen trade as well as for agricultural and industrial activities. Indeed, its importance compared to its neighbours during the Middle Ages can readily be seen in the 1379 Poll Tax when it was valued at 59 shillings, whereas Huddersfield was valued at 19 shillings and four pence. It was also home to many of the important families of West Yorkshire such as the Saviles, Thorntons, Hoptons and Beaumonts. To this day many of the fine homes that they built

can still be seen. During that time many of the local men perfected their skills with the longbow at the butts at Battyeford near Warren House. It appears that the district was not lacking when it came to producing valiant men-at-arms during times of strife. With the impending Spanish invasion in 1586, Mirfield was to provide nine pike-men. In 1642 Sir Thomas Fairfax wrote the following to the Constable of Mirfield: 'all that be of able bodyes from the age of 16 to 60 to repair to Almondbury on Saturday with all weapons they can procure and provisions for five days'. He concluded with a dire warning to the constable to fail at his peril. There appears, however, to be no record of the constable's response to either the General's request or his threats.

For much of our knowledge of the life of Mirfield in the 18th century we can thank the Revd Joseph Ismay. Vicar of Mirfield from 1735 to 1778, he kept a detailed journal, from the pages of which we glean that in 1755 the district had 100 pairs of looms worked by 200 people, and that 400 were employed in carding, spinning and other associated occupations. He also tells us that, 'the men and boys employed themselves in the Christmas holidays in hunting the squirrel which gives them violent exercise in the woods and affords them excellent diversion'. Of the River Calder he informs us that it produced, 'salmon, trout, smelts, graylings, dace, perch, eels, chub, parbles [sic], and gudgeon, and about it are found wild duck, widgeon, teal, coots and several sorts of water hens, especially in great frosts'. In the winter of 1772 the country experienced great frosts and the Revd Ismay tells us in his journal that, 'The country was seized with so great a freezing that people did skate on the Calder all its length from Mirfield to Brigg House and carts and horses did pass freely across without danger thereto.'

On 1 December 1745 the inhabitants of Mirfield were put on their guard as they learnt that the Jacobite Army was approaching. Clothes and provisions were safely hidden in the Mirfield Moor coal-pits as a precaution in the event that the marauding Scots were to sack the town. Revd Ismay reported in his journal that few women attended church on that day 'for want of apparel'.

While digging the foundations of a new house at a place called Snake Hill, workmen came upon a grisly sight. They had uncovered a pit containing the skeletons of what was thought to be the 140 men, women and children who had died during the plague that struck the town in 1641. It is believed that the source of this pestilence was a woman who had brought it with her from the South of England. A stone memorial can be found at the parish church which states 'it pleased God to correct ye Parish of Mirfield'. John Wesley once described the people of Mirfield in his diary as 'A wilder people I never saw in England…' So perhaps they were in need of some correction! It would be a mistake, however, to conclude that these were a Godless folk. Indeed this was far from the truth. In 1732 Tamar Lee, the wife of a local

A gravestone in the church grounds tells a tale of murder – an aged couple and their serving girl were cruelly murdered in their own home by Patrick Reid and Michael McCabe, two Irishmen, who had been in the neighbourhood selling small wares. Reid was executed at York and McCabe was transported for life.

Congregationalist, ventured on the dangerous journey to London. She set off, riding on horseback along roads notorious for thieves and highwaymen, on her mission to obtain funds for a new church. Later in the century John Wesley opened Mirfield's first Methodist chapel. The first Baptist meeting was to be held in Mirfield and it was in this town that the first Baptist church was opened in 1830. The Moravians were to build a church at Mirfield in the 18th century. Today the town is known as the home of the Community of the Resurrection and two of its co-founders, Bishop Gore and Bishop Frere, are buried in Mirfield. The Community was originally founded in Oxford in 1892 but moved to Mirfield six years later. They purchased Hall Croft, which was a mansion built by Thomas Hague Cook in 1871. A church was begun in 1911 and took nearly 27 years to complete. Designed by Sir William Tapper, with its verdigris copper roof, it has now become a famous landmark.

In 1830 Miss Margaret Wooller leased Roe Head, a Georgian manor house, from the Marriott family. She opened it as a boarding school to accommodate up to eight boarders. The Brontë sisters were all educated there and the eldest sister Charlotte Brontë was to return as a teacher. She even taught her other two sisters there. It was while at Roe Head that Charlotte obtained background information on the Luddites for her novel *Shirley,* and Emily was to write three of her poems. In 1838 the school was relocated to Healds House on Dewsbury Moor. Today Roe Head is a centre for the education and care of severely physically disabled children and adults. Prior to the English Civil War the Mirfield Grammar School (now known as The Mirfield Free Grammar) was built. Its first teacher was the curate of the parish church, Revd Samuel Peart. In 1667 Richard Thorpe of Hopton Hall gave the school an annual endowment of £5, so that 15 poor children could be educated 'till they could read English well'.

The successful growth of industry in Mirfield can be attributed to readily available supplies of water and coal. Writing in the 18th century, Revd Ismay informed us that there were three corn mills in Mirfield. Within less than 100 years the number of mills had grown considerably. Like many of its neighbours, Mirfield was heavily occupied with textiles, and the blanket industry in particular. Engineering and mining were also important sources of income for the town.

SLAITHWAITE

Pronounced 'Slawit' by the locals, Slaithwaite is a small town near Huddersfield. It is the home of the Moonrakers, so called after an amusing incident which dates back to 1802: a couple of wily smugglers from Slaithwaite had set up a highly profitable business selling whisky and rum. Barrels of spirit were brought in barges along the canal. One day while smuggling the barrels they were disturbed by a patrol of soldiers. The smugglers quickly slipped the

A bridge at Slaithwaite.

barrels into the reeds by the side of the canal and continued on their way, to return later under the cover of night with large garden rakes to retrieve the barrels. Working quickly in the bright moonlight, it was not long before they were disturbed yet again. The soldiers asked them what were they doing, to which they replied, 'Can't you see? The moon has fallen into the water and we're raking her out.' The soldiers walked off laughing and called the pair 'Silly Moonrakers!'

Typical of many textile towns in the Colne Valley, this unpretentious township appears the most unlikely place to find a spa; however, this is what Slaithwaite became and for a time its mineral waters were compared with those of Harrogate. First piped in 1825 by Richard Varley, the sulphur and iron spring water attracted visitors from great distances. The Victorians strongly believed that the mineral-rich spring waters had marvellous health-giving properties. Spas, where they could drink or bathe in the waters, became extremely popular.

By the end of the 19th century the town had developed into a major attraction, and the Slaithwaite Spa & Hydropathic Establishment Ltd had built swimming baths, a bandstand, a grand hall, bowling green, tennis courts and pleasant gardens. There was even a portable photographic studio where the visitor might have a pictorial keepsake taken of their visit to the spa.

During World War Two the buildings and gardens of the spa were requisitioned by the War Office to train soldiers. After the war the spa hall was bought for demolition, and there followed many years of neglect. In 2004, however, its fortunes changed when a group of volunteers and Kirklees Council combined their efforts and have been gradually improving the Spa Park. They have rebuilt walls and planted wildflowers, and they have even installed a viewing platform looking out over the river, where herons and kingfishers might be seen.

Running through the centre of Slaithwaite can be found the Huddersfield Narrow Canal,

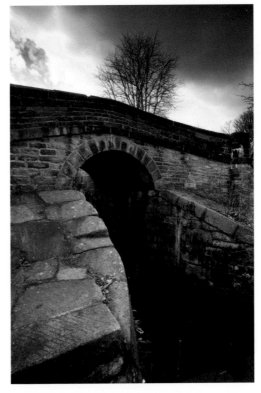

*Far left:
Slaithwaite Spa.*

*Bridge of
Huddersfield
Narrow Canal.*

Derelict building on the Brontë Way.

which links Huddersfield with Ashton-under-Lyne in Greater Manchester. Construction of this canal began in 1798 and finally opened in 1811. Although a relatively short canal, being 20 miles long, it lays claim to having the longest, highest and deepest tunnel in the country. The Standedge Tunnel extends for three miles, and due to its narrowness there is no tow path. This meant that boatmen were forced to negotiate the tunnel with their own muscle power while the towing horses had to be led over the hills. Using a method known as 'legging', they would travel through the tunnel lying on their backs and pushing against the sides and roof of the tunnel with their feet. This was a back-breaking task, taking four hours to complete, and it must have been a great relief to see the light at the end of the tunnel.

Opposite: A clearing storm on the Brontë Way.

AFTERWORD

So our brief journey has now come to an end, and as you have seen West Yorkshire has so much to offer. I have only scratched the surface of the history of this great county and there is so much more to explore. History is not an exact science but is open to debate, interpretation and opinion. The records and documents that have been left, which give us our insights to the past, have perhaps to a larger part been coloured by views and prejudices of those who compiled them: there is a Latin proverb that says 'history is written by the victor'. Perhaps that is so, but it has also been written by the scribes and clerics, and by the monuments, buildings and structures that the people have constructed by their own hands. If we want to understand our region and its past, then we need to take the time to look around us – for our history surrounds us. History is not static, for it is constantly being added to, and what we do today will one day be the material for future historians. This is what makes history exciting and full of surprises.